Marks of Christian Maturity

Other books by the same author:

Day by Day with George Duncan
It Could Be Your Problem
The Life of Continual Rejoicing
Living The Christian Life
Mastery In The Storm
Pastor and People
A Preacher Among The Prophets
A Preacher's Life of Jesus
The Renewing Spirit
Wanting The Impossible
Week by Week with George Duncan
Preach the Word

Marks of Christian Maturity

Becoming the kind
of Christian God wants you to be

George Duncan

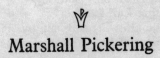

Marshall Pickering

Pickering and Inglis
Marshall Pickering
34-42 Cleveland Street,
London, W1P 5FB

First published in 1986 by Pickering and Inglis Ltd
Part of the Marshall Pickering Holdings Group

Reprinted in 1989

ISBN: 0 551 80689 5
Phototypeset in Linotron Plantin by
Input Typesetting Ltd, London
Printed and bound in Great Britain by
Courier International Ltd, Tiptree, Essex

*Dedicated to Catherine my wife
and partner in the work for
forty-six years.*

**All royalties to go to T.E.A.R.
Fund for the Catherine Duncan
Memorial Project in Calcutta.**

Contents

Introduction: Quality is what counts

Upon a recent visit to speak at the Keswick Conventions in Japan I ventured to remind the Japanese that there had been a time when in Britain if we saw the words 'Made in Japan' on anything in the shops we never bought it. The goods were cheap, badly made, wouldn't last, and were just not worth buying. I then went on to say that I felt that the Japanese had learned an important lesson, namely that if they were to win the markets of the world then quality was essential. Canon Harry Sutton when speaking to the Ministers' Meeting at the great Filey Christian Holiday Crusade reported that a recent survey showed that 15% of people in England now went to Church. Now what was meant by the words 'went to Church' was not made clear. It might simply be that for most of them 'C of E' meant 'C and E', 'Christmas and Easter'! But the survey showed that another 12% wanted to go. They were looking through the door, through the windows, they wanted to come in, but something was keeping them out, and that was the 15% who were already there!

In my long association with the Keswick Convention, not only in Britain, but also throughout the world, I have suggested that the question we ask and try to answer at a convention is not the question 'Am I a Christian?' That is the question to be faced in an evangelistic Crusade or Church Mission, but the relevant question is 'What kind of a Christian am I?' Am I the kind of Christian that God wants me to be, the kind of Christian that God in Christ has made it possible for me to be, the kind of Christian the world desperately needs to see me to be?

In this book I have put together some of the messages that deal with various aspects of this question in the light of what the Bible has to say. The late distinguished

Baptist minister of Charlotte Chapel, Edinburgh, the Rev Dr Graham Scroggie, whose D.D. from Edinburgh University was a tribute to his outstanding ministry, once said about Christian standards of living, 'There is so much awkward piety, blundering goodness, and unattractive sanctity.' These messages have not only been preached, most of them, at the Keswick Conventions in England, but also in many other lands where I have found that the spiritual needs are so often basically the same, and where the grace of God revealed in Jesus Christ is sufficient to meet every need of the human heart.

It is my prayer that in this form they may be a help and blessing to those who may read them, even as the messages in the mercy of God seem to have helped the thousands who have heard them throughout the world. The greatest debt I owe is to those who have sustained and helped me by their prayers, that debt is one that I can never repay, but their reward will lie in the blessing that God in His mercy may have added to the preaching of His Word.

I want to add my thanks to Sheila Pile and to my daughter-in-law Jennifer who have both helped in the preparation of this book.

1: Am I truly a Christian?

Having said in the Introduction that we are *not* trying to answer the question 'Am I a Christian?' I *have* to ask and answer that question in the first message. The reason is quite simply that the question 'What kind of a Christian am I?' cannot be answered unless the one trying to answer the question *is* a Christian! One of the purposes of conventions like the great Keswick Convention is that it is 'for the deepening of the Spiritual Life of the Christian believer.' But the life cannot be deepened unless that life is present.

I have included two messages, the first is titled 'Becoming a Christian' and the second 'Being a Christian'. The first message is based upon the text that helped me as a schoolboy of eleven and a half years of age to understand that while being the son of a minister, going to church every Sunday, reading my Bible and saying my prayers when I remembered, having been baptised as a baby were things that Christians might do, none of them would actually *make* me a Christian. This note is one that is struck usually on the first Sunday evening meeting in the big tent at Keswick, and is sounded out throughout the week at the evening open-air services held in the Market Square, where the witness is designed primarily for the tourists and casual by-standers. The second message on 'Being a Christian' was given over the worldwide service of the BBC on the occasion of the Centenary Convention in the year 1975. It is really a summary of all that the Keswick stands for, and of what the Bible has to say, put in the simplest language possible. I find myself concerned how some of our learned theologians seem to delight in making everything so difficult for the ordinary person to understand. Some

11

of them seem to imply that before you can be a Christian you have to be a theologian, whereas our Lord said you have to become a child. I am glad of that!

Becoming a Christian

'Behold I stand at the door and knock, if any man hear my voice and open the door, I will come in to him and sup with him and he with Me.' Rev. 3:20.

One of the most famous of all religious paintings is Holman Hunt's painting of Christ as 'The Light of the World'. One of the two or three original paintings hangs on a pillar in the south aisle of St Paul's Cathedral in London. Christ is depicted as a king, for He is wearing a crown. In His left hand He is holding a lantern, and His right hand is raised as He knocks at a closed door which is overgrown with weeds. Underneath are the words of our text which inspired the painter.

Right away, however, we run into two difficulties. The first is raised by some theologians whose thinking is dominated by their particular concept of the sovereignty of God. It is unthinkable to them that a sovereign God should have to stand humbly waiting for mere man to consent to His request! I would submit with the greatest possible respect that these good men have overlooked what lies at the heart of the revelation of God made in Christ, which is a revelation of the *grace* of God, *not* of His sovereignty. When John assessed what his contact with His Lord had meant to him he wrote, 'The Word was made flesh and dwelt among us and we beheld His glory, the glory as of the only begotten of the Father, *full of grace* and truth'. The divine majesty and glory of Christ was seldom seen when He walked this earth — just an occasional glimpse, on the Mount of transfiguration and in the garden at the moment of His arrest. But what a picture of divine grace we have here! He *is* King, He *is* sovereign Lord, but *in grace* He stands, and waits, and knocks!

The second difficulty is that these words are addressed

to a church, the church at Laodicea. Were they therefore already Christians? But how could they be if Christ was excluded from their lives? The Bible makes it quite clear 'He that hath the Son hath the life, he that hath *not* the Son hath *not* the life.' In the opening verses of this chapter the risen Christ describes the Church in Sardis as having 'a name that thou livest and art dead.' Surely it is possible to have the label of Christian, to have the label of a Church, of a denomination, a name that goes with some office held in a church, without being the possessor of the life! So let us turn with confidence to this wonderful picture drawn by Christ Himself that brings out so beautifully the sheer simplicity of the way to become a Christian. Don't be put off by its simplicity, it had to be simple, simple enough for the youngest child, or the simplest mind to understand!

A picture that is arresting

I want to suggest to you that here we have *a picture that is arresting*. It is the Christ who is speaking, who is standing at the door — 'Behold *I* stand at the door and knock,' I am arrested by two things. In the first place I am arrested by *the presence of Christ* at the door. If some people were to be found at the door of our home in Sussex I would not find their presence arresting or amazing. If I found some of my children or grandchildren, I would be delighted but not amazed. If I found some of my friends standing at the door I might well be pleased but not necessarily amazed or arrested. But if one day when a knock came on the door, I looked out through the window to see who might be there, I saw a Rolls-Royce with the royal standard flying from it, and a well-known figure of a lady standing outside the door and recognised that it was Her Majesty the Queen, I would be amazed! But who is this that stands, and waits and knocks? It is none other than Jesus Christ, the Son of God, the one who died for my sins upon the cross and who now would come and dwell in my life by His Spirit to be what I need, my Saviour and my Lord. Does this not amaze you, does this not arrest you?

Becoming a Christian is far more than going to Church, is more than receiving the sacraments, is more than saying the creeds, it has to do with Christ. So I find my self arrested by the presence of Christ.

But there is more to this picture that is arresting. I find myself arrested by *the patience of Christ* at the door. 'Behold *I stand*. . .' He stands and He waits for me to answer that knock. Here it is that the *grace* of God is revealed. Christ could break down the door, but He does not, He stands and waits. Man created by God was created with a will to choose. For Christ to force His presence would be to violate the integrity of the personality of the man God created, so He stands and waits. We find ourselves asking, 'How long has He been standing?' 'How long will He continue to stand?' The sound of His knocking is something that surely we all have experienced at one time or another.

If we have had the privilege of being brought up in a truly Christian home, we must surely have heard the sound of His knocking there! We have heard it as we have attended Sunday School and Bible class, as we have sat under the ministry of the Word of God faithfully proclaimed. We have heard it as we have passed through various experiences of life, either experiences of great joy, or of deep sorrow, through times when we have had to face the inadequacy of our own resources. We have heard it as we have watched the lives of others who have been true Christians and who have taken the step of welcoming Christ into their lives and we have sensed and seen the difference that His presence has made. Yes, we have heard the sound, but we have kept Him waiting and for how long? For weeks? For months? It may even be for years, and still He stands! But Scripture holds a note of warning and there are at least two verses that come to mind with such a note of warning. In Genesis 6:3 we read that God says 'My Spirit will *not always* strive with man.' Now He may be striving, but '*not always*'! It was these two words heard in a sermon in one of my churches that brought a young girl out of her bed and on to her knees when she suddenly realised that He might not wait to suit her convenience! The note of warning is found also in Isaiah 55:6 when Isaiah says 'Seek ye the Lord *while He may be found*, call ye upon Him *while He is near*. So we have looked at a picture that is arresting!

A promise that is assuring

I want us then to note what I have called *a promise that is assuring*. 'If any man hear my voice and open the door, I will come in'. There are two things to be noted here and to which I must give careful attention:

(i) *The Word for which Christ waits.* That is the word of welcome, of desire, of decision. Notice that little word 'if'. '*If* any man *hear* my voice *and open* the door.' Then it is possible for us not to hear, and if we do, not to heed the voice, and therefore not to open the door. But I like that phrase 'if *any man*'. Then the offer is inclusive of any and of all, young or old, weak or strong, wise or simple, rich or poor, good or bad, black or white, 'if *any* man hear my voice.' Here is that blend of discovery of desire and of decision for which Christ waits! No-one reading these words is excluded. But the welcome must be extended from us, we must want Him to come in, and we must ask Him to enter. It is the Christ that we face, it is the Christ that we need, it is the Christ that we ask into our hearts and lives. We don't become Christians by chance, but by choice. It was the challenge of choice with which Joshua faced the children of Israel, '*choose* ye this day whom ye will serve' (Joshua 24:15). Yet this need for a choice, for a decision is something from which many people will turn away in disgust. Apparently we can and do make choices and decisions in any other area of life, except when it comes to our relationship with God! I can decide what I am going to be, whom I wish to marry, what car I am going to buy, where I am going for a holiday, what I am going to eat, anything and everything is a matter of choice and of decision, but *not* in the sphere of religion! How inconsistent we can be, how hypocritical! Yes, there is the word for which Christ waits.

(ii) *The Word on which faith rests.* 'I will come in.' Some-

15

times people will ask the question, 'Supposing I do ask Christ to come into my life how do I *know* that He comes?' The answer is quite a simple one, I know that He comes *because He said He would*! What more do I want than His Word? It is not a matter of my feelings, but a matter of His faithfulness to His own word. It is not a matter of my goodness but of His grace. There is an old chorus that some of us learned to sing when we were children which puts the issue simply

I'm safe because I'm sheltered
By Jesus' Precious blood,
And I'm sure *because He promised*
And He cannot break His word!

I am well aware that there are some Christians who would say that it is presumptious for any one to say 'I am sure'. But does God want us *not* to be sure? Listen to what the Bible says in 1 John 5:11 ff. 'These things have I written into you that believe on the name of the Son of God, *that ye may know* that ye have eternal life. This life is in His Son, and he that hath the Son, *hath* the Life, and he that hath not the Son hath not the life.' God does not want us just to think, or to hope, God wants us to *know*! I love that story told of an incident in the life of the Emperor Napoleon. He was reviewing his troops and was on horseback when suddenly his horse bolted: The Emperor's life was in danger. A soldier dashed from the ranks of the troops and brought the frightened horse under control and so possibly saved the Emperor's life! The Emperor then spoke 'Thank you, *Captain*.' Whereupon the soldier accepting his on-the-spot promotion went back, not to the ranks of the ordinary soldiers from which he had dashed to the rescue of his Emperor, but to where the officers were standing. Immediately they challenged him and said, 'What are you doing here? Get back to the ranks!' The man replied 'I am a Captain now,' and turning and looking towards the Emperor who was watching the whole incident, the soldier concluded '*He said so*.' Yes, we can be sure because 'He said so,'

'*I will* come in.' We have seen here then a picture that is arresting, a promise that is assuring.

There is one more thing we need to note, and that is that here we read of:

A presence that is abiding

We read that Christ says that He will come in, but there is no word of Him going away. When He comes He comes to stay! Another chorus from my childhood days will help us here, I wonder if you have ever heard it, sung it, and meant it?

> Into my heart, into my heart,
> Come into my heart, Lord Jesus,
> Come in to-day, *come in to stay*,
> Come into my heart, Lord Jesus.

Think of *the difference His presence will make in my life*. The sharing of a meal in the east was symbolical of friendship, of the forging of a bond that could not be broken, a bond which was to be lasting. A meal shared was symbolical of everything being shared. I will be able to share everything with Him, and He will want to share everything with me. This mutual sharing will be the basis of this new life. I will be able to share my failure, and find His forgiveness; I will willingly admit my foolishness and revel in His wisdom; I will be ready to admit my weakness and will prove the wonder of His strength. My fear will be replaced with His courage, my selfishness will be replaced by His love. What a difference His presence will have in my life.

But still more than even that. I can count on *the permanence His presence will have in my life*. The whole weight of Scripture bears witness to this security. 'I will never leave thee nor forsake thee', 'I have loved thee with an everlasting love', 'My sheep will never perish.' 'Nothing can ever separate us from the love of God.' 'Goodness and mercy will follow me all the days of my life', and then even when I face what we call death 'I will fear no evil for Thou art with me.' I want to end by quoting some lovely verses written by Bishop Handley Moule when Bishop of Durham. They could be someone's prayer now while reading these words. If by any chance you have discovered that you are not a Christian, that you have never received Christ into your life, why not use this lovely hymn and make your choice now.

Come in, oh come, the door stands open now,
I knew Thy voice, Lord Jesus, it was Thou.
The sun has set long since, the storms begin,
'Tis time for Thee, my Saviour, Oh come in!!

Alas, ill-ordered shews the dreary room,
The house-hold stuff lies heaped amidst the gloom.
The table empty stands, the couch undressed,
Ah, what a welcome for the Eternal Guest!

I seek no more to alter things or mend
before the coming of so great a Friend,
All were at best unseemly, and 'twere ill
Beyond all else to keep Thee standing still.

Come not to find, but make this troubled heart
A dwelling worthy of Thee as Thou art.
To chase the gloom, the terror and the sin,
Come all Thyself, yea come, Lord Jesus in.

And Jesus said 'I will come in.'

Being a Christian

Broadcast on the World Service of the BBC centenary
Keswick Convention 1975
'To me . . . to live . . . is Christ'

I am speaking to you from one of the loveliest parts of England, from the town of Keswick in the English Lake District. Keswick is a town situated at the northern end of Lake Derwentwater, lying under the shadow of Skiddaw, one of the higher mountains in this part of England. Scot though I am, I find it difficult to argue that Scotland is lovelier than England when I find myself surrounded with that peculiarly soft beauty and colouring which is so characteristic of this part of Cumberland.

I am sure that it was no accident, but rather in the will of God, that here one hundred years ago an Anglican vicar and a Quaker layman invited Christian people to come together for a time of quiet waiting upon God. The purpose was quite simple and clear: it was to enable them to seek unhurriedly what God's will was for their lives, and what provision God had made to enable them to fulfil that will. And so in 1875 six hundred people gathered, little realising that they were witnessing the beginning of something that would have a spiritual influence of incalculable power that would reach literally to the ends of the earth.

There is so much hurry in life today, it is good to slow down, to stop even, to think, to evaluate, to learn, to decide. There is so much noise in the world today, it is good to be in a quiet place to listen for other voices, voices that we have not been able to hear, or had time to hear; to listen above all to the voice of the living God, to find out what He has to say, and then to go and do it. There is so much ugliness in the world today, ugliness and vileness which are the product of man's own evil doing, it is good to come into a place of indescribable beauty and to realise that the purpose of God is to bring loveliness into living, for did He Himself not say that this was His purpose, to 'beautify the meek with salvation,' by His saving, healing and transforming acts for men and in men through Christ.

What is the heart of the message which has been sounded out from this Convention throughout the past one hundred years? It is, of course, simply the message of the New Testament, which is there for every man to read in the Word of God; a message about a Person, Jesus Christ. We seek to come face to face not only with what He has done for man through His death upon the cross, but with what He can do in man through His risen life received and then released in the receptive and obedient heart; leading on to what He is able to do through men who are ready to go out in obedience into this tragic world in which we live, and to share with others what Christ has done, and can do, for us all.

This full-orbed and balanced experience of Christ has been summed up by that greatest of all Christians, St. Paul, in six unforgettable words, which in English at least are words of one syllable each, and should therefore not be beyond the understanding of the youngest or simplest of us. St. Paul wrote to the church at Philippi — 'To me . . . to live . . . is Christ' (1:21).

I want to suggest to you that there are three facets of the Christian experience that are made abundantly clear here. In the first instance, to be a Christian:

1. *Is something personal. 'To me. . .'*

A Christian is not someone who is thinking in terms that are just denominational or theological, though both denomination and theology have their part to play. He is thinking in terms of a personal relationship between himself and Jesus Christ. There are two aspects of this personal relationship that become clear from the New Testament. This relationship is personal for the Christian because it is:

(*a*) Personal in *his acceptance of Jesus Christ*. I have to accept Christ into my own heart and life by His Spirit, and to accept Him personally for myself and by myself. In John 1:12 we are told, 'To as many as received Him, to them gave He the power to become the sons of God, even to them that believe on His name.' In Revelation 3:20 the risen Christ is speaking to a church-so-called which was a church in name only but not in nature, and He says, 'Behold, I stand at the door and knock: if any man hear my voice, and open the door, I will come in.' It is, personal in my acceptance of Christ; knowing Him to be who He is, the Son of God and the Saviour of the world, the One who died on the cross to bring men into a new relationship with God in spite of their sin; the One who rose again and who lives today to bring into men's hearts new resources that will transform their lives into the likeness of His own.

This relationship is also personal to me because it is:

(b) Personal in *my allegiance to Jesus Christ*. This one who is my Saviour is also my Sovereign and my Lord. This means that there will not only be a new adequacy in my life, but a new authority. When Paul wrote to the Christian church at Ephesus he described the principles which had determined their conduct before they had become Christians, and those principles still determine the conduct of those who are not Christians today. He wrote, 'Ye walked according to the course of this world,' or in other words, you did what everybody else did. And again, 'Ye walked fulfilling the desire of the flesh and of the mind,' you did what you wanted to do. What everybody does, what I want . . . how accurate and how up-to-date is the diagnosis of the Word of God! But when Christ came into the life of Paul everything was changed, and the question he asked on the Damascus road tells us how immediately he was aware that the pattern of living would never be the same again, 'Lord, what wilt *Thou* have me to do?' To answer that meant getting to know the mind of his Lord, and then getting busy doing the will of his Lord!

Personal in my acceptance of Christ; personal in my allegiance to Christ. Something personal, 'To me. . .' But Paul goes on to say, 'To me *to live*. . .' Then being a Christian:

2. *Is something practical*

It has to do with living, not just with going into a building for an hour on Sunday; not just forming devotional habits of prayer and Bible study that may last for five minutes each day. It has to do with living sixty minutes in every hour, twenty-four hours in every day, seven days in every week, fifty-two weeks in every year, and for every year of my life. 'To me to *live* is Christ.' Then two things will follow. The first is this:

(a) That *every moment of my life will be spent with Christ*. This means that everywhere I go, and whatever I do, and all the time, Christ will spend the moments with me, and I will spend the moments with Him. What

21

an answer this is to that basic form of loneliness of spirit from which every one of us suffers and to which not one of us can find the answer apart from finding it in Christ. It is He alone who can enter into the very depths of my personality and, dwelling there by His Spirit, put an end to that loneliness which so often makes life so hard for so many. But it will mean more: it will mean:

(b) That *every matter in my life will be shared with Him.* And if our reaction to that is, 'But there are some things that I could not possibly share with Him' then the reply to that is quite simply, 'Then you would be better without them.' It is significant, isn't it, that one of the pictures of the relationship between Christ and the Christian found in the Word of God is that of marriage. Christ is spoken of as the bridegroom; and the church, in the true sense of the meaning of that word, is described as the bride.

But the real basis of a true and happy marriage, surely, is the sense of 'togetherness' in which everything is shared and in which there are no secrets. If we share our lives with Him, let us not forget that He will share His life with us. And this will bring a meaningfulness to life that nothing else and no-one else ever can. His purposes will become ours, and His resources will become ours. So tremendous is the change that St. Paul describes it in these words, 'If any man be in Christ (and therefore Christ be in him), he is a new creature.' For him life becomes something utterly and wonderfully new. 'To me. . .' something personal; 'to live. . .' something practical. 'Ah!' says someone, 'that sounds wonderful, but of course I could never hope to live that kind of life; that sort of standard is far beyond anything that I could ever hope to attain. . . But Paul has not finished; he ends by saying — 'To me . . . to live . . . *is Christ!*' Personal . . . practical . . . and *possible*!

Yes, being a Christian:

3. *Is something possible*

'To me to live *is Christ*.' Then the Christian life is Christ living His life out in the Christian. Paul does not say that to him to live is to follow Christ, to serve Christ, or to try to be like Christ, but quite simply, 'to me to live *is Christ*.' It was not a life that he was attempting to live, but a life that he was allowing Christ to live in him! So we find him writing elsewhere of 'Christ Who is our life,' Col. 3:4. So many folk are trying to live the Christian life without having it, and others are attempting to live the Christian life instead of allowing Christ to live it in them.

I want to close by making two comments for our encouragement. The first is that this life is: (a) *available to all*, because Christ is available to all. Nothing is plainer from Scripture than this, that the love of God which took Christ to die upon the cross for the sins of the whole world (cf. 1 Timothy 2:3–6 and 2 Peter 3:9) offers to that same whole world all that Christ had achieved by His death and will achieve through His risen life. In Romans 5:10 Paul writes, 'if when we were enemies we were reconciled to God by the death of His Son, much more being reconciled we shall be saved by His life?' The new relationship is ours through the death of Christ; the new resources are ours through the life of Christ, present in our lives by His Spirit, available to all. And therefore this Christian life on this level is: (b) *attainable by all*. What I cannot do, He can. What I do not have, He has. What I lack, He supplies. My foolishness will be corrected and controlled by His wisdom. My selfishness will be mastered by His indwelling love. My fears will be conquered by His courage. My weakness will be undergirded by His strength. To live the Christian life is to live the new life a pauper lives when she marries a millionaire!

This is what Keswick is all about. Trying to find out what is stopping us from living this life, and putting it right. Finding out just exactly what the resources are that are available in Christ to enable us to live this life. Facing the cost in terms of obedience, and making up our minds as to whether or not we really are willing to pay the price. Learning how the Holy Spirit will make everything real in our lives if we are prepared to allow Him to do in us what He wants to do, and be in us what

He wants to be. Looking round at the others who share the same life with us, to see how differently we may be equipped but how dependently we will live and work together! Looking out upon the world in all its confusion, its utter bankruptcy, and seeing just where and how we can get involved.

Someone has put it this way — The Christian is not someone who stands wringing his hands and crying out, 'See what the world is coming to,' but someone who stands raising his voice and crying out, 'See what has come to the world.' And what is it that has come to the world: just Jesus Christ in all His adequacy and authority. He has come to the world. Has He come to you; and if He has, have you welcomed Him, have you received Him? Have you released Him in your heart and life to do what He wants to do in you, with you, and through you, so that you too can say with Paul, 'To . . . to live . . . is Christ.'

2: Facing up to failure in our lives

A 'Keswick' Convention has been likened to a spiritual clinic, when the patient goes in to see the doctor alone. Indeed a famous Scottish preacher, the late Rev. Alexander Frazer, used to say that the only convention that ever achieved anything was a convention of two! The first task of the doctor is to try and find out what is the matter with the patient and where the trouble is to be found. And so it is that we have to bring our lives into the searchlight of God's Word and truth, and that can be a somewhat disturbing experience. Sin and failure in the lives of Christians is a denial of the message of the gospel that we believe in. When we recall the words spoken to Joseph about the Child that Mary was to have: 'Thou shalt call His name Jesus for He shall save His people from their sins', we are inclined to limit that saving work of Christ to our being saved from the guilt and the just punishment of our sins, but the words spoken to Joseph are not to be limited to that. Christ came to save us not only from the guilt of our sins, but from their grip on our lives. He came to save His people (and if we pause to ask who *they* are, we get the answer in John 1.12. 'To as many as received Him, *He gave the right and the power to become the children of God.*') from their sins, from the penalty, *and* from the power, *and* one day from the very presence of Sin. If we are living defeated lives then we bring the whole message of the gospel into disrepute, and the name of Jesus Christ is brought into dishonour. I remember hearing of two missionaries in the East African Revival who were challenged by some African Christians who were much more open in what they had to say than we might be: 'We think you should go home', they said to these two missionaries! Shocked, the missionaries replied in amazement, 'Why?' 'Well, you say that you have come to tell us that Jesus can save us from our sins, but He is not saving you! You can't get on together!' So then there is a call for Christians to take action about the failures that we so often tolerate so casually in our daily lives, a call to repentance! What counts is not so much what we may appear to be amongst the other Christians, but what we are at home, in the office, on the wards, in the classroom in the factory. So in the next two messages we take a look at two aspects of failure, at the measure of our obedience, and then at forgotten vows which still have to be fulfilled.

Broken Promises . . . unpaid vows
Eccles. 5:1–7

One of the more colourful figures that have graced the platform at the Keswick Convention in England was the late Dr Donald G. Barnhouse, an American Presbyterian Minister from Philadelphia. One little phrase of his has remained in my mind and memory: 'The way to up is down.' I cannot recall the context of those words, but I assume that they were based upon the words of Christ when He said, 'he that humbleth himself shall be exalted.' In looking at areas of failure in Christian living I would like to consider a similar phrase based upon the passage of scripture that I want us to consider in Ecclesiastes 5:1–7. The phrase that I have in mind in 'the way to on, is back.' In other words that before we can make any further headway in our Christian experience there may be something in the past that calls for action. You may remember the words of the risen Christ to the Church at Ephesus recorded in Revelation 2:5. 'Remember therefore from whence thou art fallen, and repent, and do the first works.' You may recall too the words of Christ in Matt. 5:23, 'If thou bring thy gift to the altar and there rememberest that thy brother hath ought against thee, leave there thy gift before the altar and go thy way, first be reconciled to thy brother, and then come and offer thy gift.' 'The way to on, is back!' You may recall the words that came to Jacob in Gen. 35:1 when God said to him 'Arise and go to Bethel and dwell there'. For Jacob too, the way to on, was back!

The passage in Ecclesiastes deals with one aspect of spiritual experience which is surely something with which we are all familiar, namely the vows that we make to God. This has to do with our response in intention and resolve to God's revelation of Himself and His will and truth. We begin with noting something here that comes to us with a sense of surprise, I have called it:

God's plea for restraint: (cf.v2)

'When thou goest to the House of God . . . be not rash with thy mouth to utter anything before God.' Here the Old Testament ties up perfectly with the New Testament for one of the characteristics of the methods of Jesus Christ was the restraint He continually imposed upon would-be disciples. If we read Luke 14:25–33, we find that after stating the terms of discipleship and indicating that if the terms were not met then Christ said quite plainly three times you 'cannot be my disciple.' Again in Luke 9:57–62, the same tactics were employed. How different from the approach that so many of us make today when we tend to try to make the terms of Christian discipleship as easy as possible in our attempt to gain new followers.

I want us to note (a) that *the reasons for this were simple*. The reasons have to do with the circumstances under which we so often do make our vows to God. We make our vows so often *when we are in trouble*. In Ps. 66:13 and 14 we read what the Psalmist has to say, 'I will pay Thee my vows which my lips have uttered and my mouth hath spoken *when I was in trouble*.' But troubles can pass, and with the passing of the trouble the desire to implement the vow passes too! It would be a fascinating study in any group of Christians to examine their experiences and to find out just how true this has been. It may have been a time of sickness, of sorrow, of financial stress, that in our need we turned to God and vowed our vows. But we sometimes make our vows not just when we are in trouble, but when we are *under the stress of some strong emotion*. But just as troubles can pass, so emotions can subside, and when the emotions subside so does the desire, the intention to keep the vow. I am not decrying the place of emotion in religious experience. Prof. Henry Drummond who exercised such a powerful influence upon the student world of his time makes this comment about emotion. He quotes the words about Peter after his denial of His Lord where we read that 'he went out and wept bitterly.' Professor Drummond's comment is 'this short sentence settles for ever the place of emotion in true religious experience.' But it is not enough if the emotions are stirred, the mind must be informed and the will obedient. The whole personality must be involved. So we note that the reasons behind God's plea for restraint were simple.

We note further (b) that *the results of this were sound*. We see this particularly in the quality of discipleship that the Master secured. He left only a handful of men and gave them the colossal task of being witnesses to the uttermost parts of the world. And what a job they made of it! When they came to Thessalonica they were described by their enemies as 'those that have turned the world upside down.' He picked and trained a small team but what an impact they made in the power of the Holy Spirit. Surely there is nothing more badly needed to-day than a high quality of Christian witness in the same Power of the same Spirit. Someone has said that while the Church is looking for better methods, God is looking for better men. On a recent visit to Japan I pointed out to the Japanese Christians that I could remember the time when if you saw the words 'Made in Japan' on something that was for sale you just didn't buy it. It might be cheap but it was of the poorest quality, it wouldn't work reliably, and if it did it wouldn't last. I suggested that the Japanese nation had learned its lesson that if it was going to win the markets of the world with the products of its industry, then quality had to have the first priority in their thinking! I suggested that today in other lands the picture had changed completely. Now if you wanted to buy a reliable car in the UK you might be tempted to buy Japanese. If you wanted a reliable television set you would think of one made in Japan, and so with cameras and watches! What about the Christian Church in its effort to capture the markets of the souls of men. What is the quality of goods that the world can see in the shop windows of our lives?

The second thing to note in this passage from the book of Ecclesiastes is what I have called:

God's preference for refusal

In v5 we read 'better it is that thou shouldest not vow, than that shouldest vow and not pay.' What a strangely unexpected word to hear. 'Better it is that thou shouldest not vow.' This calls for two comments and the first is this (*a*) that *there is no greater tragedy than this*, 'that thou shouldest not vow,' and the tragedy is in the lack of any response at all to the love of God. God will do everything that love can do to get the response of obedience and faith from the hearts of men, the Holy Spirit will strive with man, the vision of truth will be given, the circumstances will be created, all and everything will be done to evoke a response but all to no avail! I remember hearing of a mother with a severely handicapped child on which she lavished all that her love could do. The days, the weeks, the months passed, the years passed but there was never the slightest sign of recognition or response. A close friend one day said to her, 'I don't know how you can do it.' To which the Mother replied. 'If only she would respond once and call me 'mother', it would be worth it all!' If that is true of human love, how much more true it must be of the love of God. If we were to pause and think back, all of us can recall times when it was like that with us, when we failed to respond to the voice of God. There is a phrase in use among certain theologians who speak of 'irresistible grace'. But I don't find that in my Bible. I find Stephen, the first martyr, on trial for his faith charging his accusers, 'Ye do always *resist* the Holy Spirit.' I find the Saviour grieving and weeping over the Holy City with the words, 'How often would I, and ye would not.' And again He speaks, 'Ye will not come unto me that ye might have life.' Nothing irresistible there! But what a tragedy it is when this is so!

But there is more on which to comment here, for if there is no greater tragedy than what we find here of not responding to the strivings of Divine love, the further comment must be made namely (*b*) that *there is no greater travesty than this* 'that thou shouldest vow *and not pay.*' This is what God in His wisdom is seeking to avoid, that of lying to God. In his old religious classic 'Holy Living and Holy Dying' Jeremy Taylor gives as the first rule in holy living 'Don't lie to God.' True Christian discipleship is not a matter of saying the right words with our lips, it is a matter of carrying out those words in the nitty-gritty business of our lives in this difficult and often hostile world. It was Dr. Leslie Weatherhead the well-known Methodist preacher, (with whose theology I differ from time to time,) who wrote, 'to call Jesus Lord is orthodoxy, to call Him Lord, Lord, its piety, but to call Him Lord, Lord, and not to do the things which He commands is blasphemy.' It is this travesty that God would avoid, the travesty of hypocrisy. God is saying 'I would rather that you said nothing, than that you said something that you did not mean to carry out.' However, we have not finished yet with what this passage has to say, let us read on.

The final message that leaps out of this page of my bible is this, for I find here:

God's passion for reality. cf. v4.

'When thou vowest a vow . . . defer not to pay it, pay that which thou has vowed.' We need to note two things here, firstly *the assumption that God makes.* '*When* thou vowest. . . .' God does not say 'if', but 'when'. The assumption is that at some time or another all men do make some vow to God. If that is so then it is true of all of who read these words. Either in the past vows have been made, or in the future vows will be made. What an unfolding of human experience and of Divine grace there would be if in any given congregation the stories could be told of vows that have been made. How different the vows would be, at what different times in our lives. Vows made maybe at our wedding, at the birth of a child, at the loss of a loved one. To what different places we would be taken, to the quiet of a hospital ward, or the hush of some great gathering of Christians. How many different voices would be heard, the voices of a thousand preachers, some of the voices long since silenced in death, other voices we still hear! What memories would be revived, memories of crushing anxieties, of overwhelming joy and happiness, of great grief. Yes, the vows have been made! God is right to assume that the vows have been made *'when thou vowest a vow. . . .'*

Secondly, we note *the action that God wants.* 'defer not to pay it . . . pay that which thou has vowed.' or as the RSV renders it 'Do not delay paying it.' We do well to recall the words of the psalmist to which we have already referred when he says 'I will pay Thee my vows which my lips have uttered and my mouth hath spoken when I was in trouble.' The vows were indeed *'my* vows', the lips were indeed *'my* lips', and the mouth that spoke the words was indeed *'my* mouth'. Yes the vows were made, but they have never been paid. What was the vow? Was it the vow to become a Christian? But you are still not a Christian. Was it a vow to forsake some known sin in your life? But the sin is still there. Was it a vow to follow some pathway to which the Lord was leading? But the path is still not followed. Is this the simple word of the Lord to someone reading these words today? 'Pay that which *thou* hast vowed.'

Our final thought, however, must be to sound a note of warning. One of the most solemn statements about God's dealings with men comes in the Book of Genesis where God speaks in these words, 'My Spirit shall *not always* strive with man.' There is a danger of thinking that we can deal with this issue in terms of responding at our own convenience, when it will suit us! As if we think that we are the only people involved, but we are not. When Christ said 'no man cometh unto Me except the Father draw him,' I don't believe that He meant that God draws some and not others, He does not say that. He does say that the drawing constraint of God's Spirit will be involved too. According to Paul the natural man is naturally hostile to God, and it takes the constraint of the love of God to break that hostility down, so Christ makes it plain when He says 'I if I be lifted up *I will draw all men.*' It is not a matter of making my response when it suits me, but when God is giving me the opportunity as He seeks to draw that response from me by His Spirit's striving. That opportunity may indeed be frequently given to me, but '*not always.*' The moment may come when it is my last opportunity, when it is a matter of 'now or never'. I remember reading of the experience of a man who was a collector of birds eggs found on the cliffs in some parts of Scotland. On one occasion when he was hanging by his rope where there was an overhang he saw a nest on a ledge that he could only reach by swinging himself towards it. It took a number of such swings, each of gathering momentum before the ledge was within reach, but at last he landed on the ledge. In a moment of forgetfulness he let go the rope which swung back away from the ledge. Instantly he knew the danger he was in, as the rope swung back it came just within his reach, but it would not the next time. The decision was immediate, forgetting about the eggs he leapt and caught the rope and climbed back to safety. God's rope may be within your reach at this very moment, but it could be your last chance. The word for you is the word 'jump!' — do it now. 'Pay that which thou hast vowed' — 'pay it now!'

What is the measure of our obedience?
'*By faith Abraham obeyed God. . .*' Hebrews 11:8

'Revival consists in a new obedience.' So wrote Charles Finney. Any study of the major truths in the Word of God indicates that obedience runs through them all like a golden thread. The question I want us to ask ourselves is what is the measure of our obedience? If it plays such an important part in the doctrines that lie at the heart of our Christian faith and experience, how vital it is that the measure of our obedience should be such as satisfies the demands of our God. Let us note first how obedience *is* linked with truths that are prominent in our thinking today. In some quarters we hear a great deal about election? but what is the purpose of our election? In 1 Peter 1:2, we read that we are 'elect unto *obedience*'! Are we thinking in terms of the ministry of the Holy Spirit? Then Paul tells us in Eph. 1:13 that when we believe we were '*sealed* with the Holy Spirit.' Dr Jowett, a former occupant of the pulpit of Westminster Chapel in London comments 'a seal implies contact, imparts likeness and indicates *ownership*!' Ownership surely involves *obedience*! There is a lot of talk in some quarters about 'love', but what is the mark of true love? Our Lord tells us in John 14:21, 'he that hath my commandments *and keepeth them*, he it is that loveth me.' What is the secret of true blessedness or happiness? The final beatitude in Rev. 22:14 tells us 'Blessed are they that *do His commandments.*'

The question is however about the measure of our obedience. When studying at the University of Edinburgh for my MA degree, the pass mark in most subjects was set at 50% although in two out of the seven subjects the pass mark was 60%. When one of my two sons was studying to become an airline pilot he told me that the pass mark was set away up into the 90% range! I thought that was pretty tough, then I thought, 'If I got into a plane and knew that I had only a 50% chance of reaching my destination I would want a pass mark set not 50%, nor even 90%. I would want it at 100%! 'What percentage marks the quality of our obedience to God? Someone once said that Christians today are treating the ten commandments as they would treat the questions in an examination paper: 'Out of ten questions only five are to be attempted!' For our guidance let us then look at the obedience of Abraham. The story is set out in Genesis chapters 12 and 13.

I want to begin by noting what I have called:

The revelation that was given to Abraham

Right at the very heart of this man's obedience lay the
fact that God had revealed Himself to Abraham. The
revelation was a twofold one.

In the first place there was a revelation of *the person
of God*. If we turn to the New Testament we find this
recorded in Acts 7:2, in the opening words of the defence
of Stephen the first martyr. He begins with these words:
'Men and brethren, hearken, the God of Glory appeared
unto our Father Abraham when he was in Mesopotamia
before he dwelt in Charran.' It is vital to note that *the
basis of faith is knowledge*. I suppose that the most
frequently quoted verse about the faith of Abraham and
the one most open to misunderstanding is in Heb. 11:8,
where we read 'By faith Abraham when he was called,
obeyed and he went out *not knowing* whither he went.'
The conclusion that so many draw is that faith has some
kinship with ignorance, like the small boy who when he
was asked 'what is faith?' replied 'faith is believing what
ain't!' But if we note exactly what the scripture says we
note that while the Bible says that Abraham did not
know *where* he was going, it does not say that he did not
know *the One* at whose command he was going. God had
revealed Himself to Abraham and that revelation was the
basis of his faith and obedience. The basis of faith for
the Christian is the same. So Paul makes it clear in
writing to the Romans when he asks, 'How shall they
believe in him of Whom they have not heard? So faith
cometh by hearing, and hearing by the preaching of
Christ.' I know the position of some who hold that faith
is 'a gift of God.' I would only submit that the scriptural
evidence for that is too shaky for that position to be
maintained. Calvin rejects that interpretation of Eph.
2:8. And the only other verse which at first sight seems
to support that position is Phil. 1:29 but most fail to
note that the word for 'give' in that verse is not the
ordinary word for give as a gift, it is a word which is
rightly translated in the NEB granted '*as a privilege*'. The

NIV translator has unwisely punctuated his translation of Eph. 2:8 to suit his own theological position! The punctuation there in my judgment would be more correct if it read, 'by grace, are you saved through faith, and that (i.e. being saved through faith) is the gift of God.' Now you cannot have faith in someone you do not know, but if you know someone who is worthy of your faith and trust, then you respond with faith and obedience! The Christian has in Christ a fuller revelation of God's saving grace than Abraham had, and therefore should respond with a fuller and more completely obedient faith. As Dr Alexander McLaren has said 'Those who know what is meant by faith in a promise, know what is meant by faith in the Gospel; those who know what is meant by faith in a remedy, know what is meant by faith in the blood of the Redeemer; those who know what is meant by faith in a physician, a friend or an advocate know what is meant by faith in the Lord Jesus Christ.'

But the revelation given to Abraham was not only a revelation of the person of God, it was also *a revelation of the purpose of God*. There were two sides to this: 'Get thee out of thy country and from thy kindred, and from thy father's house unto a land that I will shew thee.' There was *the obedience for which God was calling*; 'and I will make of thee a great nation, and I will bless thee and make thy name great and thou shalt be a blessing . . . and in thee shall all the nations of the earth be blessed.' *There was the outcome for which God was planning.* There is a strange similarity here, is there not, with the purpose of God in Christ through the church? 'You shall receive power after that the Holy Ghost is come upon you and you shall be witness unto me unto the uttermost part of the earth.' Acts 1:8. 'All the families of the earth' were involved in the outcome of the obedience of Abraham; 'the uttermost parts of the earth' have been involved in the obedience of the Church. We recall too the words of our Lord in the temple when He said in John 7:37-39. 'If any man thirst let him come unto Me and drink. He that believeth in Me out of his innermost being shall flow rivers of living water.' This spake

He of the Spirit!' Rivers of living water that would flow *out*, they would flow on and on, touching life after life, reaching land after land! The purpose of God in the gift of the Holy Spirit was not so much that Christians could have a wonderful time, but that rather that with His enabling they would do a wonderful job! Through the prayers we offer, through the words we say, through the gifts we give, through the lives we touch, through the letters we write, through the servants we send, the uttermost parts of the earth would be reached so that the declared will of God 'Who will have all men to be saved' might be accomplished. What a purpose!

But then a shadow falls across the path of this man of faith as we note what I have called:

The reservation that was made by Abraham

We read in Gen. 12:4. 'So Abraham departed as the Lord had spoken unto him, *and Lot went with him.*' God's demands had been crystal-clear, there was to be a complete break with his native land, the people of his nation, and with all his relatives. It was in that final demand that Abraham made his personal reservation. He was willing to leave his native land, the people of his nation, but he wanted to take at least one of his relations with him, and that was Lot. Again and again the scripture records this action, in Gen. 12:5. we read 'Abraham took Sara his wife *and Lot* his brother's son,' in Gen. 13:1 'Abram went up out of Egypt *and Lot* with him.' In v5 of that same chapter we read '*and Lot* also.' It is a matter of speculation why Abram did this. Was it for the sake of fellowship? The New Testament speaks of 'righteous Lot' in 2 Pet. 2:7! Was Sarah, Abraham's wife not really in sympathy with her husband in this crazy step he was taking? We don't know the answer, all we do know is that there was a reservation in the obedience that Abraham gave to the voice of God. We can note two things about this reservation.

In the first place *the reservation that Abraham made was deliberate*. He knew precisely what he was doing. It is however important to note that there *had* been a very real response to the will of God. Abraham's obedience of faith had been costly in the extreme, it had no doubt involved immense sacrifice and very considerable effort. I believe that this is true of the majority of true and believing Christians. We are *not* indifferent to the voice and will of God. We too have made a very real response. For us too it has no doubt at times been costly, has called for sacrifice and great effort on our part. But what was true of the obedience of Abraham has been true of our obedience too, there has been a real response but there have been reservations too. We are prepared to obey God *so far*, and not all the way. There has been retained in our lives something, or maybe someone that God has made it clear should not be there! The disobedience of Abraham was quite deliberate, so has ours! It may be that in the mind of Abraham was the thought 'in due time I will part with Lot, but I am going to hang on to him for the time being!' But surely delayed obedience is disobedience! As someone put it, 'Obedience means at once'! One of the many memorable phrases heard at the Keswick Convention over the years that has stuck in my mind and memory is this: 'If Jesus Christ is not Lord of all, He is not Lord at all!' It was, I think, the late Archdeacon H. W. Cragg who told the story one year of the small girl who was in no hurry to come down to breakfast. Her mother called her with the words. 'Hurry up, breakfast is ready.' To which the child replied, 'All right, Mummy, I'm coming.' Some minutes passed and there was no sign of her coming, so Mummy called again 'Hurry up, darling, breakfast is ready.' Back came the same reply, 'All right Mummy, I'm coming.' After some more time has elapsed there was still no sign of her daughter, so again the mother called, 'Hurry up, darling, breakfast is ready!' For the third time the answer came back, 'All right Mummy, I'm coming!' To which Mummy replied, *'Stop coming, and come*! Is this the position in some of our lives, we intend to obey God, but not yet? We need to face the fact that delayed obedience is disobedience.

Abraham's disobedience was not only deliberate but *the reservation that Abraham made proved disastrous.* It is not long before we find him wandering into Egypt where lying and deceit led to him being treated with contempt by the Egyptians! But I wonder if something more serious lay behind that straying right out of the will of God. Was his fellowship with his God affected? I note that in Gen. 12:1–3 God has a lot to say to this man; in v7 God has less to say; in v.8 God has nothing to say. We are warned in the Psalms 'if I regard iniquity in my heart the Lord will not hear me' Ps. 66:18. It seems to make sense that fellowship with God is affected by disobedience in our hearts. Surely all of us have memories of our childhood of acts of disobedience that made us uncomfortable in the presence of our parents! Our relationship remained, but our fellowship was at an end! I wonder if someone reading these lines is in precisely that situation at this very moment. There was a time when fellowship with God through His Word was a blessed and wonderful reality, but for long enough that has not been so any more! Is disobedience the cause? So we find in the story of Abraham a reservation that had been made by him, it was deliberate and it proved disastrous. But thank God the story does not end there!

I want us to note finally what I have called

The restoration that was found by Abraham

The final chapter to our study leads us to see how his obedience which had been only partial, at last becomes perfect and total. There are two stages in this experience of grace given to Abraham. First of all we can see *the way in which we find God working in his life*. We read in Gen. 13:3 'Abraham went on his journey from the south even unto Bethel unto the place of the altar which he had made there at the first . . . and there Abraham called upon the name of the Lord.' The man is on his knees again and is found at prayer. That was a wise thing to do. Sometimes the way on is at first the way back! And the cry for help and mercy which must surely have gone up from the heart of Abraham is the one prayer that surely God will always hear and heed! The answer may seem at first to be a strange one, for things got even more difficult for Abraham! In v7 we read that trouble brought Abraham face to face with Lot. 'Trouble broke out between the herdsmen of Abraham's cattle and the herdsmen of Lot's cattle.' It seemed as if God was bringing Abraham face to face with the real issue at stake. He was, if you like, rubbing Abraham's nose in his failure to deal with Lot. Surely all of us who have persisted in disobedience have had the same experience when God in His mercy and grace has brought us face to face with the matter about which God has a controversy with us. We just have not been able to dodge the issue any longer. Maybe the very fact that you are reading this very chapter in this book is just such an instance of the way in which we find God working in our lives. The second thing to note is this.

I see here *the word for which I find God waiting from his lips.* Abraham was facing the issue of Lot yet again. What would he do this time? I wonder if God ever holds His breath! If He does then He most have been holding it at that moment. At last Abraham speaks, but what will he say? Listen! He is speaking to Lot in v.8. 'Let there be no strife I pray thee between thee and me and between my herdmen and thy herdmen, for we be brethren. Is not the whole land before thee? *Separate thyself I pray thee from me!*' I am sure that when those words were at last spoken on earth there must have been a deep-sounding 'Amen' in heaven. And the Lord who had had less and less to say to Abraham until he had nothing to say, now lets him know that the channels of communication that had been clogged and closed were now open again! The pent-up waters break through in a torrent of words, in a flood of grace, cf. ch. 13 vv14–17. 'Lift up thine eyes and look from the place where thou art, northward and southward, eastward and westward, for all the land that thou seest to thee will I give it and to thy seed for ever. And I will make thy seed as the dust of the earth, so that if a man can number the dust of the earth, then shall thy seed also be numbered. Arise, walk through the land in the length of it and in the breadth of it, for I will give it unto thee.' But *when* did the Lord say all this? When did the full purpose of God for and through His servant begin to be fulfilled again? We find the answer in v14, *'after that Lot was separated from him.'*

Is God waiting for a similar totality in the obedience of those who name His name today? Is God giving to someone reading these words a similar chance as that given to Abraham? Has the word that finally and at last came to the lips of Abraham come to our lips? We have seen that the way in which God was working in his life may well be the way in which He is working in our lives. But has the word for which God was waiting to fall from his lips, fallen from ours? Just supposing that Abraham had missed the opportunity God had given to him! Surely we would never have heard of his name at all! He would have stepped out of the will and purposes of God not simply for him, but through him for the whole world. Supposing he hadn't grasped the opportunity supposing we don't grasp the opportunity!

History has never been a strong point with me although British history was included in my Master's degree, but of American history I know even less so I cannot vouch for the truth of this story, but it was written as having truly taken place. It happened we are told when the American Civil War was coming to an end. The generals of the North were meeting the generals of the South to negotiate terms of peace. The generals of the South were prepared to cede this piece of territory and that, but each offer was greeted with a shake of the head. When the final offer was made, the general from the North in charge of the proceedings shook his head and then laid his hand upon the map spread out on the table between them and said 'Gentlemen, *my Government must have all.*' If Christ is not Lord of all, He is not Lord at all! The obedience for which He asks is a total obedience in every area of my life, and all the time!

Many years ago I was in charge of the Young People's Meetings at Keswick and we usually had a theme chorus for the week. One year we had as our theme chorus one which seems to sum up everything we have been thinking about in this study of obedience. These are the words:

Jesus, Lord and Master,
Love Divine has conquered,
I will henceforth answer, 'Yes',
To *all* Thy will.
Freed from Satan's bondage,
I am Thine for ever
Hence forth all Thy purposes
In me fulfil.

3: Is it possible to have victory over sin?

If we were to believe the words of some of our great hymns, the answer to that question would be an emphatic 'yes'. How lustily we sing that great hymn, 'Oh for a thousand tongues to sing my great Redeemer's praise!' And what about the verse. 'He breaks the power of cancelled sin, He sets the prisoner free!' It is one thing to sing it, it is a very different matter to prove it in the battle of life. We face a powerful trinity of evil called 'the world, the flesh and the devil.' As Bishop Taylor Smith used to describe that trinity 'the world with all its allurements, the flesh with all its subtlety, and the devil with all his experience.' What hope has the Christian when facing forces like these? The answer is surely, 'No hope at all!' And yet the Scripture bears witness to the fact that the life of victory is possible. 'If I the Son of God shall make you free, you shall be free indeed.' So said Christ! 'In all these things we are more than conquerors,' so writes Paul! 'My grace is sufficient for Thee, for my strength is made perfect in weakness.' So speaks the risen Christ! 'These things write we unto you that ye sin not.' So writes St. John in his first epistle. We said above that the answer to the question 'what hope has the Christian to live triumphantly?' is 'No', but that has to be qualified. If the Christian cannot live triumphantly, *Christ can!* I remember one of the choruses that used to be sung in the Young People's meetings held at the Keswick Convention. In those far distant days when I was in my teens, the meetings being held after the last Evening Meeting in the Big Tent, and presided over by the late Mr. A. Lindsay Glegg. It contained the words — 'On the Victory side, on the Victory side, no foe can daunt me, no fear can haunt me, on the Victory side.' Then came the second half which held the secret to the experience of the first half of the chorus — 'On the victory side, on the victory side, with Christ within, the fight we'll win, on the Victory side.' Note the little phrase *'we'll win'* The 'we' means 'Jesus and me'. What I cannot do *He can*, and He will if I let Him! This is not sinless perfection, the Bible says quite plainly that 'if we say that we have no sin, we deceive ourselves and the truth is not in us.' No, it is not sinless perfection, but it is perfect deliverance in Christ. As the great Methodist preacher, the late Dr. Sangster has written, 'Any Christian can safely say at any time, *I need not sin now.*' Why? Because Christ is the Victor, and what I cannot do He can! But what if defeat has taken place, can victory come back? The second of the messages that follow tells how it can!!

From difficulty, through discovery into doxology
2 Corinthians 12:1–10

I want to examine one of the most treasured passages amongst all the writings of St. Paul; treasured by Christians who have known something of difficulty in their lives and who desire to find God's answer to their problems in Christ. Among the earliest of the addresses I ever gave at Keswick there is one on this passage of Scripture. I titled that message on which God's blessing graciously rested, as 'The Discipline of Disappointment'. Under that title the message has been published as a booklet and widely distributed, and is also included in one of my books.

But one of the exciting things about the Bible is that one can come back to a passage and find new light where one thought one had seen all the light there was to be seen! And so it was that in later years when I was studying the passage again a new title came to my mind and a new message, a fuller message I believe. I titled it

'From Difficulty, Through Discovery, Into Doxology'. I have once again done my homework, I have read my translations of this particular passage, and read my commentaries to see if there might be some fresh light upon the passage, a fresh outline maybe that would sum up its content and meaning for us. We might have called it — 'the conflict of the soul, the concern of the saviour and the coming of the song' — but I feel to do this would be to take away from the earlier outline that God gave me, and so I am going to go back to that familiar outline and maybe bring some fresh thoughts following the main structure of that message.

In a sense what we will be doing will be rather like being invited to go round a beautiful garden that we know well but in which we can always see something fresh, a garden whose beauty and fragrance is one that fills our hearts with praise and thanksgiving. This analogy is apt because the word translated 'paradise' in this passage means a walled garden, and Paul apparently feels that the experience God gave him was rather like being shown round a beautiful garden full of fruit and flower and fragrance. So let us come to the message of these choice verses when Paul, recalling an experience that happened to him some fourteen years previously, shares its meaningfulness with the Christians at Corinth. I believe that this passage may enable us, in the words of Dr. Stuart Holden, to transform what he calls 'the thorn pain into the triumph song'.

This is possibly the most intimate and most revealing passage in all the epistles. The great apostle draws aside the veil of natural reserve and shares with the Church at Corinth and with us one of those hours of spiritual crisis that stand like milestones along the pilgrim way. Let us note three aspects of this passage:

A. There is difficulty here

How easy it is for us to think that great Christians have no problems, that those who appear to us to be spiritual giants have an easy time. They seem to know all the answers, their lives seem to display an easy mastery, their words are words of authority and experience, their service for God bears a quality and an effectiveness that make our efforts seem poor and amateurish. And in the consciousness of the magnitude of the problems that we have to face and the feebleness of our efforts to solve them we look almost enviously at such lives and we say, 'It is all very well for him'; 'It is all very well for her'. I wonder how often people must have said that about Paul — 'it's easy for him'. This passage shows us how wrong such an attitude could be for us, for here in the heart of this the greatest of all Christians there lay a problem that seemed to defy all solution, a pressure that to him was almost unbearable. Let us look then with reverence and let us learn.

As we consider Paul's difficulty we note first of all: (a) *A pressure that seemed unhelpful*. He calls it 'a thorn in the flesh, the messenger of Satan to buffet me'. What precisely it was we do not know but from this description we can gather enough to let us see something of what it meant to Paul. Commentators differ as to whether this was a reference to something physical or something spiritual. Paul uses the words 'the flesh' in both senses, and I personally am convinced that here this is something spiritual! Paul is referring to the flesh in the sense of the old carnal nature within. It may have had physical involvements but basically Paul is dealing with something spiritual here. In its origin it seemed satanic — he calls it 'the messenger of Satan', in its object it seemed to be a major hindrance in his life and work. He calls it 'the messenger of Satan to buffet me'. Both the RSV and J. B. Phillips translate this as 'to harass me' and the NEB translates it 'to bruise me'. The word is a strong one for it means to buffet with a fist. Here was something utterly frustrating, something which left Paul bruised and beaten. Paul was harassed by it, frustrated by it. I wonder if there are any harassed Christians reading these words! In its outcome this thorn in the flesh seemed to make Paul conscious of the old nature within, to arouse it, to awaken it, to make Paul aware of it. It tended, as we might say, to bring out the worst in him. Do we know anything of this kind of situation? We have no doubt that the Devil is behind it; we find it utterly frustrating; if only it wasn't there then everything would be wonderful, but it is there and every time we are confronted by it the old nature — the flesh — is aroused to activity within and brings out the worst in us, our temper, our pride, our lust, our self-will.

The other aspect of this difficulty lay in: (b) *A prayer that seemed unheard*. v8 'For this thing I besought the Lord thrice that it might depart from me'. Paul did what all of us do about problems and pressures like this — he prayed about it, and behind that prayer was the conviction in the mind of Paul that this thing had to go. He did not simply pray but he prayed with the specific intention 'I besought the Lord thrice *that it might depart from me*'. This thing was a hindrance and in the mind of Paul it had to go. It was a hindrance in his life, it was a hindrance in his service — he would be far better without it. Paul was quite clear about that. Have you and I ever prayed that kind of prayer? We want something, someone, some situation, to be dealt with by God. It has simply got to end or our whole life as Christians will be spoiled, our testimony and usefulness will be ruined.

But as Paul prayed it seemed as if his prayer was unheard — once he prayed, twice he prayed, three times he prayed, and one can imagine the intensity of desire that lay behind Paul's praying. Was there a tinge of complaint, almost of reproach? Why did he have to ask the Lord three times that it might be taken away? How often have you and I prayed about our problems, the pressures in our lives that have seemed unhelpful? Far more times maybe than that. Is there however a lesson that we need to learn? Paul started praying and *then he stopped praying*. I wonder if God interrupted him: I wonder if God wants to interrupt us. In v9 we read '*and He said* unto me' and the tense there is the perfect tense. It means, he did say and has been saying to me ever since. Has God got to remind some of us of a need to listen, instead of going on asking? What would God say to you, what will He go on saying to me?

If there is difficulty here then:

B. There is discovery here

As Paul listened, so he learned. When Paul stopped talking, God started speaking, and God spoke of two things. First of all Paul discovered (a) *The unrecognised purpose of God* v7 'lest I should be exalted above measure' or as J. B. Phillips translates it more dramatically 'to prevent my becoming absurdly conceited'. Twice Paul records these words. It would seem as if the lesson was well learned. There was one danger that dogged the steps of this greatly used man, this greatly blessed Christian. A danger that it would seem Paul never sensed but God sensed it, and God now shares it with His servant, and the danger was simply that of pride. With such a record behind him how easily Paul could have become proud, and had he become proud he would therefore have become useless. Spurgeon has a great sermon on the text 'supposing Him to be the gardener'. The gardener knows the right soil for each plant and sometimes it may be the soil of sorrow and of suffering. It was because God knew, that He planned things this way and permitted 'the messenger of Satan to buffet' His servant. This was permitted to achieve one purpose only but that was a vital purpose. It was there to keep Paul a humble and therefore a usable Christian, 'lest I should be exalted'.

I don't know what may be the special area in your life or mine that God knows to be in need of special care. It may be there is something lacking in our character, something lacking that could therefore endanger our witness: or it may be there is something that needs to be preserved. But always behind the pressure there is the purpose of a God of perfect love, perfect wisdom and perfect power. Many of you will remember the poem written by Amy Wilson Carmichael of Dohnavur. She recalls in this poem an experience that came to her when she was three years old, but so vivid was the experience that it left an indelible mark upon her mind and she recalled in these words:

Just a tiny little child, three years old
And a mother with a heart all of gold.

Often did that mother say,
'Jesus hears us when we pray
For He's never far away
And He always answers'.

Now that tiny little child had brown eyes
And she wanted blue instead, like blue skies:
For her mother's eyes were blue,
Like forget-me-nots. She knew
All her mother said was true,
Jesus always answered.

So she prayed for two blue eyes, said goodnight,
Went to sleep in deep content and delight.
Woke up early, climbed a chair
By a mirror. Where! Oh where
Could the blue eyes be? Not there!
Jesus hadn't answered.

Hadn't answered her at all. Never more
Could she pray. Her eyes were brown, as before
Did a little soft wind blow?
Came a whisper, soft and low
Jesus answered. He said, 'no'.
Isn't 'No' an answer?

Little did that little girl of three years old with her brown
eyes know that God's purpose for her lay in India. In
India where she was to become the 'mother' of thousands
of unwanted temple children, where she was to *become*
an Indian! She needed those brown eyes and God knew
it, although she didn't. Have you ever met an Indian
woman with blue eyes? No, their eyes are always brown,
and God had given her the eyes that she needed. The
unrecognised purpose of God!

But there is something more here that Paul was to
discover and that was: (b) *The unrestricted plenitude of
grace*. What did God say to him and keep on saying to
him? 'My grace is sufficient for thee' It is important to
note that this is not a promise it is a statement 'My grace
is sufficient for thee', therefore there is no need to escape
from the pressure. Paul, you want this thing to go —

not only would that be unwise but it would be quite unnecessary! There is no need to escape when God's grace is sufficient and there is therefore no room for excuse. So often we make the pressure of some persistent problem become an excuse for lowering our standards. We say, 'you would need the patience of Job to keep your temper'. But you don't need the patience of Job when you have the patience of Jesus! 'My grace *is* sufficient.' This is a present tense statement. Grace is never experienced in anticipation but at the moment of need it is there, and it is sufficient.

There is difficulty then: there is discovery: and finally there is:

C. There is doxology here

And here the thorn pain is transformed into the triumph song. If this experience is to be ours let us follow Paul here and note: (a) *How Paul's attitude is changed.* 'Most gladly therefore will I rather' is translated by the NEB as 'I shall therefore prefer'. What would Paul prefer? What would Paul rather have? Well surely he is simply saying that he'd rather that this pressure stayed! Would we dare to follow him here? We have seen how Paul prayed that this thing might be taken away from him, and now instead of praying for it to be taken away he is saying he'd rather that it remained. I don't know what the pressure is in your life that seems so desperate that you want to be rid of it — it's such a hindrance it simply must go; but could you, dare you; could I, dare I, look at that thing and say to God, knowing that something is involved in it of infinite worth and value, 'we'd rather it stayed'? Paul's attitude is changed and: (b) *Paul's acceptance is complete.* He says, 'There was given to me' and of course the gift was from the Lord's hand ultimately. But a gift has to be accepted. It is not enough for us to submit to these circumstances, we must be willing to accept them! And Paul accepts this gladly because he has found that the gift is a gateway to an experience of Christ's sufficiency that could never be his any other way. v9: 'Most gladly therefore will I rather glory in my infirmities that the power of Christ may rest upon me.' And here is his final testimony, v10: 'I take pleasure in infirmities, in reproaches, in necessities, in persecutions, in distresses for Christ's sake: for when I am weak, then am I strong.' Some time ago I came across a poem which puts this in words that to me are quite unforgettable. The poem is entitled:

Accepted!

Accepted! From Thy hand, dear Lord, I take
This hurting thing and bear it for Thy sake.
Nor bear it only, but in Thy dear name,
Thy strength, Thy power, to love it Lord, I claim;
To love it till from struggles, toil and tears,
The likeness of Thy life in me appears.
Accepted! From Thy hand this thing I take,
Lord, make it glorious for Thine own name's sake!

The man in whose life victory came back
Judges 13–16

There are few characters in the Old Testament that have such a hold upon our imagination as the character of Samson in the book of Judges. There are three ways in which the story of Samson has been treated, as Dr. Whyte of Free St. George's, Edinburgh, points out. There are those who treat the character of Samson purely as mythical or legendary; there are others whose treatment of the life of Samson is mystical and in some strange way they seem to be able to see in Samson a type of Jesus Christ: there are yet others who agree with St. Paul that 'All these things happened unto them for example and they are written for our admonition,' or in other words there are lessons that New Testament Christians can learn from Old Testament lives. I believe that the latter is the sensible way to approach the character of Samson and I feel that the title for our message will awaken a responsive chord in many a life, for Samson is a man concerning whose life we can say — he was the man in whose life victory came back.

I want to survey the four Bible chapters that contain the record of Samson and to find in them the four words that sum up the story of this strangely alluring and attractive character.

The first chapter in the life of Samson I would title:

Destiny

If ever a child was a child of destiny Samson was, both in his home and in his birth this was true of him. And in a very real sense this is true surely of every child of God who has been born again of the Spirit of God. You recall the words of St. Paul in Ephesians 2:10 that we are 'His workmanship, created in Christ Jesus unto good works, which God hath before ordained that we should walk in them.' There are two aspects of this element of destiny in the character and life of Samson that are worth noting: (a) *The conquest in which others would share.* In chapter 13:3–5 something of this is revealed. 'He shall begin to deliver Israel.' To understand the background to the life of Samson we need to remember the fact that the children of Israel had been delivered into the hands of the Philistines for forty years but at last it seemed that God was moving into action and the tyranny and slavery of two generations was to be brought to an end. Surely the destiny of the Christian has something in common with that of Samson, for the Christian is meant to experience not only a salvation from the *penalty* of sin but also from the *power* of sin, and to experience this not simply for himself or herself but to share this deliverance with the world. The whole New Testament echoes and re-echoes with this note of liberation in and through Jesus Christ 'If the Son shall set you free ye shall be free indeed.' Thus the note sounds forth from the gospel record. From the epistles we read of 'the glorious liberty of the children of God' and from the book of the Revelation we read that we have been 'made kings and priests unto God.' And the longing for liberation is more widespread than we think. In one of our national newspapers I read an article by Malcolm Muggeridge dealing mercilessly with the failings of the Church of England but the article ends with words of another tone. He speaks of the thirst in the hearts of men today for another and a better way of life. He writes, 'The thirst is very great much greater and more widespread than is generally supposed. There is a conscious and passionate awareness that this morally appalling and spiritually impoverished affluent society in which we live with its accent everlastingly on consumption and sensual indulgence of every kind is no better than a pigsty.' And men were not destined to live like pigs. Today, as then, there are millions, weary of servitude, men living as slaves whom God meant to rule as kings. The second aspect of the note of destiny in the life of Samson centres around: (b) *The conditions to which Samson must adhere.* In v5 we read, 'the child shall be a Nazarite unto God from the womb'. To find out what this means we have to turn back to Numbers 6:12ff. While details of the conditions and vows of the Nazarite are suggestive, the principle is decisive. The Nazarite was to be 'separated unto God from the world'. v3: 'He shall separate himself from wine and strong drink', that is to say the Nazarite would be disciplined in his appetites. v5: 'There shall no razor come upon his head', that is to say the Nazarite would be different in his appearance. v6: 'He shall come at no dead body', that is to say the Nazarite would be distinctive in his associations. We are not concerned so much today with the details of the Nazarite vow but we are concerned with the principle underlying the acceptance of these vows, namely that the Nazarite life was to be one of peculiar, special and diligent obedience to the will of God. How urgently true this is in the New Testament, and so we read there of the greatest of all Christians, the apostle Paul, nearing the end of his earthly pilgrimage and being able to say 'I was not disobedient unto the heavenly vision'. Of all things, of all principles, of all qualities, of all characteristics that are found common to men of destiny in the service of God, this quality is outstanding namely that they were men who chose to obey God rather than men.

The second chapter in the life of Samson could be titled:

Ministry

Some years ago I recall getting a letter from a friend of mine serving in the Christian Church in another land. It was in reply to one from myself in which I had asked him how he was getting on. In his reply he stated that his work was characterised by 'battle and blessing'. So it was with Samson. His ministry was first of all: (*a*) *A story of achievement*. Chapter 15 v20 tells us the length of his term of office — it lasted for no less than twenty years. That was a long time, and during that time his name was an honoured one on the lips of God's people and with good cause. His name was associated with places that had been the scenes of his triumph, places like Timnath, Ashkelon, Etam, Lehi, Gaza, Sorek. These places and the people there had good cause to remember the name of Samson. And for those that have been recorded no doubt there were scores of others whose names would be closely identified with the ministry of Samson but for the record of which there has been found no place in the book of Judges. All throughout those years 'the spirit of the Lord' had come upon Samson again and again and again, enabling him to achieve miracles of victory and triumph for his God and for his people. What he did bore the stamp of the enabling of the Holy Spirit, unmistakably, undeniably. And so it is with so many lives, some on a greater scale, some on a lesser scale. Names of churches, names of towns, of villages, are associated with their life and the impact of it. There are places that will never forget them, people that will constantly recall them, churches, homes, camps, missions, where their lives counted for God and other people knew it and noted it. Their names will never be forgotten for what the Spirit of the Lord achieved through them.

But if it was true that Samson's ministry was a story of achievement it was also: (*b*) *A story of attack*. If the name of Samson was honoured by so many, it was also hated by others; it was hated by the enemies of God, and there still are those who are the enemies of God and of the gospel of Jesus Christ. Paul speaks of such in Philippians 3:18 where he writes of those who are 'the enemies of the cross of Christ.'

My friend described his ministry as one of blessing and battle. It was so for Samson. 'The Philistines be upon thee, Samson' was the cry that he must often have heard. How often he must have been aroused by this warning shout until he was very sick of the very sound of the name Philistine. In chapter 15 v6 we read of his wife being killed by them. In chapter 15 v14 we read that at Lehi the Philistines 'shouted against him', in chapter 16 v2 we read that at Gaza they 'laid wait for him' all night. In chapter 16 v4 at Sorek they finally trapped him through Delilah.

Not only was his life one of fierce and constant attack from without but he was attacked again and again from within. Those from whom he had a right to expect sympathy and support worked against him. His first wife, in chapter 14 v16 plotted with his enemies: his own people in chapter 15 v11 complained 'What is this that thou hast done?' Everybody found him too disturbing an influence, too dangerous a man to have about the place, and so for twenty years his life was one of achievement but also of attack, and the historian records that for twenty years he judged Israel 'in the days of the Philistines', and what that final phrase meant in the life of Samson only eternity will reveal. But life is always like that for the child and servant of God. If there is to be achievement there will most certainly be counterattack. If God is going to move, the devil is going to try and move first and you and I can expect little else, for surely this was true of the life of our Lord Himself. What achievements the gospel story records and what attacks! Attacks that never ceased right up to His very dying moments on the cross itself.

The third chapter in the life of Samson could be titled:

Tragedy

Chapter 16:15–21 covers this. The tragedy in the life of Samson was not that he loved Delilah; for the Bible record does not give any indication that it was anything other than a true and genuine love for a woman. The tragedy in Samson's life however lay: (*a*) *In what he allowed*. He allowed himself to be robbed of the strength that he had received from God. The secret of this strength he himself knew perfectly well yet deliberately in a moment of weakness he allowed himself to be robbed of it. Samson knew wherein the secret of his strength lay — it lay in his obedience to his vows of which that long hair was but one outward symbol, and in allowing himself to be robbed of that he indicated that he deemed his separation to the will of God and his obedience to the will of God to be of lesser account than his acquiescence to the whim of a woman. His relationship to God was broken when he submitted to another pressure, to another's will.

I think it is worth noting that he only yielded under pressure, as we read (chapter 16 v16), 'She pressed him daily with her words, and urged him, so that his soul was vexed unto death and he told her all his heart.' When Samson woke from that fatal sleep he knew what had happened to him but he had not fully realised what had happend to his relationship to the Lord. So it is with the Christian who knows the secrets of spiritual strength and we too know when we deliberately fail to maintain the conditions of spiritual fullness. When our Bible is left unopened, when a sin remains unforsaken and unconfessed, when our prayer life is like an altar in ruins, when a temptation is deliberately yielded to, it is only too possible for us to be like Samson and to allow ourselves deliberately to be robbed of the secret of our spiritual strength.

The tragedy of Samson lay also in: (*b*) *What he attempted*. (Chapter 16 v20) His words betray this. He said, ' "I will go out as at other times before and shake

55

myself." And he wist not that the Lord was departed from him.' We cannot apply every detail of an old Testament experience to a New Testament believer. I am convinced that the teaching of the New Testament is that the presence of the Spirit never leaves a Christian but the smile of His favour may and I am convinced does leave the Christian who is disobedient and who grieves the Spirit. Samson said, 'I will go out as at other times before'. Is there a hint here that this was not the first time that he had disobeyed God, that God had been so gracious, so longsuffering, but now God's patience had reached a limit? God had been merciful in the past but this time it was to be different. Samson was conscious of the fact but not of the effect and he went out to battle as of old but he went out this time to defeat and to dishonour until we find him in chapter 16 v21 bound and blinded, a subject for scorn and ridicule amongst the enemies of God's people. Tragedy! But surely this is something that can happen to any Christian who has forfeited God's favour and who has grieved the Holy Spirit, and who in the dishonour and defeat that become characteristic of his life, becomes the object of the scorn and ridicule of the enemies of the gospel of Jesus Christ.

This however was not the last note in the story of Samson. We titled our sermon 'The man in whose life victory came back' so there is one more chapter before the story ends:

Victory

The man in whose life victory came back! How wonderfully this illustrates the truth stated in Romans 5:20 that 'where sin abounded there did grace much more abound' and so it is that we read in Chapter 16 vv23–31 of the victory that marked the closing hours of Samson's life. So great it was that in v30 we read, 'the dead he slew at his death were more than they which he slew in his life.' There are two things to examine here, two facets of the experience through which Samson passed that are recorded for our learning: (*a*) *Penitence moved him*. I am sure that two things now found a place in Samson's life that had perhaps been absent for long enough — tears and prayers. See that giant of a man with such a record destined to rule and deliver the people of God now bound and blinded, grinding corn in the prison-house. I am sure that the corn was wet and salt with tears that as the hands moved the lips moved also for we read in v22 'the hair of his head began to grow again' and although this is the record of something that was happening naturally and physically I am sure it was also symbolical of something that was happening spiritually. A heart of obedience was beating again within the breast of this broken man until we read in v28, 'And Samson called unto the Lord' God will always hear the cry of the penitent, the man in whose heart penitence moves. So we note first that penitence moved him and then secondly: (b) *Omnipotence mastered him.* Once again we see him surrounded by the enemies of his people and his God. Samson is being mocked, he is the sport of his foes, he is outnumbered three thousand to one but at that very hour victory came back for as the people mocked Samson it was Samson's God they mocked too and God moved in judgment. The point I think to learn at the end of Samson's life is that it doesn't matter how long we live but how we live. And so the record states, 'So he died with the Philistines and the dead which he slew at his death were more than they which he slew in his life. Then his brethren and all the house of his father came down and took him and buried him'. Three thousand years dissolve like mist and we find that this place in Gaza, this is the mill, this man and that man is Samson over again, only with the difference that we have sinned against a light and a truth of which Samson knew little or nothing. Should there be any Samson reading these words may Samson's prayer be your prayer and mine: 'O Lord God, remember me, I pray thee, and strengthen me. O God let the victory come back in my life for Christ's sake. Amen.'

4: Is faith 'believing what ain't'?

Many of us have a sympathetic feeling for the boy who, when he was asked 'what is faith?' replied 'Faith is believing what ain't'. Faith can seem so intangible a thing, so mystical as to be quite impossible to understand. I am sure that it is not meant to be that. The fault may well lie with some of us preachers and theologians. Have you heard of the girl to whom her mother was trying to explain something in the Bible? She interupted her mother and said, 'Mummy if you would stop explaining it, I would understand it!' Part of the confusion arises from one verse in particular: verse 8 in Ephesians 2. The problem arises from the fact that there is no punctuation in the Greek. The words run, 'By grace are ye saved through faith and that not of yourselves it is the gift of God.' It is interesting to play around with the punctuation and see how the sentence can be made to change its meaning. The NIV (Not Infallible Version!) writes the verse like this, 'By grace are ye saved, through faith – and this not of yourselves it is the gift of God.' That implies that it is the 'faith' alone that is the gift of God. Calvin however rejects this because while in Greek 'faith' is feminine in gender, 'this' here in the Greek is neuter. This suggests that the 'this' cannot refer to 'faith' alone, but reaches back beyond the word 'faith' to the word 'saved'. Change the punctuation and you change the meaning, 'By grace, are ye saved through faith, and that not of yourselves, it is the gift of God'. This means then that what grace has done is to make salvation depend not upon our works, but upon faith placed in Christ. The impossible has been replaced by the possible, because anyone can trust! I believe that this is the right interpretation of this verse, and makes faith understandable. I always think of the response that faith is, the resources that faith taps, and the results that faith sees. I know that there are those who maintain that if 'faith' is something that I do, then that means that I am saved by my works. One writer goes so far as to say that that makes me my own Saviour. But if I put my faith in a surgeon, does that make me my own surgeon?!!! That is quite absurd! My faith does not contribute to my salvation, it simply makes my salvation possible, as it enables Christ to save me, just as my faith in a surgeon enables the surgeon to save me. But the initial act of faith has to be followed by a maintained attitude of faith in Christ, a reliance upon an obedience to the One who not only died for me on the Cross, but dwells in me by His Spirit. Saved by faith, we then go on to live by faith, trusting in His wisdom that never makes any mistakes, His love that never lets anyone go, and His power that never accepts any defeat!

What it means to have faith in God
'Leave it all quietly to God my soul.' Ps. 62:1 (Moffat)

Every Christian is prepared to admit that faith in God has a vital part to play in our relationship with Him, but to many of us there is something almost unreal about faith. The Bible has so much to say about it to which we give at least our mental assent but we don't find it too easy to put what the Bible says into practice in our daily life. So many verses come to mind stressing the essential part that faith has to play. 'By grace are ye saved through faith.' (Eph. 2:8); 'Therefore being justified by faith we have peace with God.' (Rom. 5:1); 'The just shall live by faith.' (Rom. 1:17). We are told that we must 'walk by faith' in 2 Cor. 5:7. And in that great Westminster Abbey chapter in the Epistle to the Hebrews we are reminded that the secret of the great achievements of men and women of God was 'by faith'.

One of our problems I believe is due to the fact that

some of us have been taught that Christian faith is something different from the other ordinary faith that we have to exercise every day of our lives. We have been taught that 'faith' is a gift from God. I would submit that the scriptural evidence for that kind of teaching is *very* uncertain, and is not a sure basis upon which I would be prepared to base a major doctrine. I find again and again in my Bible that faith is quite simply a response to knowledge. Paul tells us quite simply that 'faith cometh by hearing and hearing by the word of God' or if you prefer the RSV, by 'the preaching of Christ'. This follows the question 'how shall they believe in *Him of whom they have not heard*?' Dr Alexander McLaren takes that position and simplifies faith and makes it more understandable when he writes 'Those who know what is meant by faith in a promise know what is meant by faith in the gospel. Those who know what is meant by faith in a remedy, know what is meant by faith in the blood of the Redeemer. Those who know what is meant by faith in a physician, a friend or an advocate know what is meant by faith in the Lord Jesus Christ.' Faith is quite simply that blend of dependence, reliance and obedience with which man can respond to the knowledge that he has received. Supposing you had been knocked down and been badly hurt in a road accident. Well-meaning bystanders might well gather round and try to help. They might want to move you, but the moment they tried to do that you would cry out in your pain, 'Please leave me alone, that hurts.' They would then draw back but would still stand around looking anxiously into your face. But supposing another face then appeared and a voice said quietly to you 'I am a doctor, can I help you?' Your reaction would be quite different. You don't know much about this person, but you know enough to trust him, he is a doctor! 'Faith cometh by hearing.' I don't believe it is a gift from God but a response from man to truth he has had revealed to him.

Phil 1:29 is sometimes also quoted to indicate that faith is given to us — but the Greek word there is not the usual word for give as a gift, but means given '*as a privilege*'!

One verse that has helped me possibly more than any other in understanding faith is the verse I have taken from Psalm 62:1. In the AV it reads 'Truly my soul waiteth upon God.', in the RSV it reads 'For God alone my soul waits in silence.' But Dr Moffatt's translation to me is more helpful than any of the others, it reads 'Leave it all quietly to God my soul!'

Let us note three very simple but intensely practical truths that we can learn from this translation. The first lesson concerns what I have called:

The wholeness with which our faith is asked to trust

'Leave it *all*. . . .' Think for a moment of (a) *The exceptions that we are prone to make.* So often we take the statements in the Word of God that call for a universal application and we immediately qualify what God's word says with a 'but'. The Bible says 'all' and we say 'all *but*. . .'. Take the problem of the forgiveness of sins. The Bible speaks of a universal cleansing from sin for all believers, in 1 John 1:9 we read, 'If we confess our sins God is faithful and just to forgive us our sins and to cleanse us from *all* unrighteousness'. But sometimes a Christian who has fallen into grievous sin will qualify that word 'all' and add 'but of course God could not forgive me my sin.' Surely when God says 'all', He means what He says!

Take again the problem of the circumstances of life that may sometimes seem unhelpful and unproductive of anything worthwhile. What does the Bible say? In my Bible I read in Rom. 8:28 that '*all* things work together for good to them that love God'. We agree in theory, but then again we immediately qualify what the Bible says by saying 'but of course what I am going through at the moment cannot possibly be productive of anything good.' I am reminded of a saying by the late Bishop Taylor Smith who put it this way. 'All things work together for good; that means not 99 things out of a hundred, but 99 *and 1*.

Take again the problem to some people of the scope of the atonement. What does the Bible say? In 1 Tim.

2:4 Paul writes of the will of God being that '*all* men' should be saved, and to make that possible Christ gave His life 'a ransom for *all*.' No, say some theologians, not all but only all the elect! But what does the Bible say, it says clearly 'all men', 'a ransom for *all*'. It is incredibly presumptuous for men to tamper with the word of God and change God's 'all' into 'all but. . .'. St John confirms what Paul writes when in 1 John 2:2 he says that in Christ we have one who is 'the propitiation for our sins, (he was writing to Christians) and *not for ours only but also for the sins of the whole world*. Was Paul telling a lie? Was John writing a lie? When John the Baptist cried out 'Behold the Lamb of God which taketh away the sins of the world', should he have said 'who taketh away the sins of the elect'? Was John the Baptist conning the crowd into thinking that Christ had come to take away their sins, while all the time He had done nothing of the kind? It is quite extraordinary to me to read in a book by a well-known theologian to find that having written that the four references in the Bible to propitiation were so important that he would quote them in full, but then when he comes to quote 1 John 2:2 he leaves out the final words of St. John, 'and not for ours only but also for the sins of the whole world'. When God's word says 'all' we must not, we dare not erase it to suit either our theology or the excuses we want to make for our low standard of Christian experience.

Take again the problem of victory over sins. What does the Bible say? In Rom. 8:37 Paul writes 'In all these things we are more than conquerors through Him that loved us.' 'In all', there is the sphere of our victory, 'we are', there is the scale of our victory, 'through Him', there is the source of our victory. Again we are faced with the challenge of another of God's 'all's.

Here in our text we are told 'leave it *all* quietly to God my soul.' And almost every one of us while prepared to trust God with many things in our lives have the dreadful habit of not trusting Him with everything, we too make exceptions and find that there are some things that we are going to handle ourselves, and go on worrying about ourselves. So we do well to go on to note that here our text speaks to us of

(b) *An instruction we do well to heed.* Let us face up to the implications of that word 'all' as it may affect us individually. 'Leave it all. . . .' If some of us have been making an exception where God makes none, why not take that matter and add it to the other things about which we have been trusting our Father God. Many years ago my own father spoke at the Keswick Convention on the words 'forgetting . . . casting . . . reckoning. . .'. When expanding on the word 'casting. . .' he looked at the counsel that Peter gives in 1 Peter 5:7, 'casting *all* your care upon Him, for He careth for you.' My father added a comment which has stuck in my mind at least, over the many years that have passed since then, he said 'casting is our part, caring is His.' 'Casting *all* your care upon Him.' 'Leave it *all* quietly to God.'

Is there something in the past that I am not prepared to trust to my God? Is there something in the present that I am not prepared to trust to my God? Is there something in the future that I am not prepared to trust to my God? You and I trust Him in so many circumstances, with so many problems, but we have not trusted Him with *all*! We have trusted Him with so much but not with everything. Today the command comes to us from the Word of God as well as from the heart of God 'leave it *all* quietly to God, my soul.' Let us think through this first lesson that we can learn from our text which speaks to us of that wholeness with which our faith is asked to trust.

The second lesson is one which is possibly even more challenging, we are told that we must 'leave it all *quietly* to God. . .' and this speaks of:

A stillness in which our faith is asked to rest.

'Leave it all *quietly*. . .'. The RSV word is 'in silence'. How does the old jingle put it? 'If we trust we do not worry, if we worry we do not trust'. There is no tension in trust!

There are two comments however that must be made here. The first is that (*a*) *There may be some progressive steps that faith may have to take*. Those who have travelled by air, will be familiar with the announcement from the flight deck to fasten seat belts because of expected turbulence! There can be a testing time for faith, or if you like a progressiveness in faith. I learned this some years ago when I read a summary of an address given at Keswick by the late Rev. Evan Hopkins, at that time Vicar of Holy Trinity Church, Richmond, and a great teacher at the Convention. He was looking at the story of the faith of the Nobleman, whose son was sick, recorded in John 4:46. I amended slightly the points he made, but the thrust of the truths expounded helped me enormously.

It is significant that there were four steps that the faith of this man took, and which so often we have to take ourselves. We are told '*he heard*', that is faith *hearing*, two things blend together here, the need he had, and the news he heard, for him faith came by hearing, and what he heard about Christ he believed, that was his response to knowledge. Then we are told '*he went*,' that is faith *seeking*, faith stirred to action, faith determined to relate the news it had heard to the need it could not resolve. Here again there would be a blending of two things, the duration of the search which must have taken time, and the desperation in the soul of the men who knew that delay could prove fatal. We can assume safely that when finally he reached the Christ, he was a desperate man. Having found the Christ we read that '*He besought Him*', that was faith *pleading*, faith on its knees, faith at prayer. But it was just at that moment when the reality of this man's faith had in one sense been proved, for it had brought him to Christ, that the quality of his faith was then probed by our Lord. He wanted to know if this man's faith was in Himself alone, or in Himself in part only, and the other part was in some sign or wonder that he was expecting to find. So our Lord spoke to him and said to him, 'Except ye see signs and wonders will ye not believe.' But the man was not interested in signs and wonders, he was concerned

64

with two things only, that he needed help, and that he believed that Christ could meet that need! That is a point we do well to consider for so many of us our faith is not in Christ alone, but in Christ *plus* something else, some sign or wonder, some great emotion or ecstasy. That was in part the heresy that was threatening the church at Colossae, that Christ was less than God and less than all!

Then we see how his faith was ready to take the final step, and this was the step that was to me at least new. For if there are some progressive steps that faith may have to take, we note here (b) *there is one decisive step that faith must finally take*. What do we read? First of all we listen to what Jesus said, 'Thy son liveth, go thy way.' Note that that was a statement, not a promise. The promises of God are usually conditional, but this was a statement, 'Thy son liveth' and it covered his need completely. Then note what the man did, we read 'the man believed the word that Jesus had spoken to him and he went his way.' Faith hearing had become faith seeking, had become faith pleading and now finally had become faith *resting*. He stopped praying and for the first time really believed the word that Jesus had spoken to him. We see the prayer that ceased and the peace that came! Quietly and simply he rose and went away with nothing more than the word of Christ which he believed. All the tension and strain had drained out of his heart and out of his face and he was now at peace. 'Leave it all *quietly* to God', the wholeness with which our faith is asked to trust is to be followed by the stillness in which our faith is asked to rest.

But there is one more truth we have not yet considered and that is:

The fulness on which our faith is asked to count

'Leave it all quietly *to God* my soul.' There are two final thoughts which hold the ultimate secret of it all and the first is (a) *the Person He is*, He is God with all the attributes of perfect wisdom, love and power! And this God is our Father for we are his children if we have been born again of His Spirit. Most of us will know John

Newton's hymn: 'Amazing Grace how sweet the sound', but I wonder how many of us know another of John Newton's hymns, the first verse of which reads:

Be still my heart, these anxious cares
To thee are burdens, thorns and snares,
They cast dishonour on Thy Lord,
And contradict His gracious word.

Another verse reads even more wonderfully with these words,

When first before His mercy seat
Thou didst to Him thine all commit,
He gave thee warrant from that hour
To trust His wisdom, love and power.

In Him we find that wisdom which never makes any mistakes, that love which never lets anyone go, and that power that never admits of any defeat. With such resources surely adequate for any situation and any need, we can enjoy the peace of God which passeth understanding!

Let us then never forget the person our God is, the One in whom our faith is placed. There is a verse of a hymn that reminds us that it is not so much our faith as the Person in whom our faith is placed that settles the whole issue, it runs like this:

Let me no more my comfort draw,
From my frail hold on Thee.
Only in this rejoice with awe,
Thy mighty grasp of me!

But in addition to our remembering the Person He is let us also never forget (b) *the People we are!* We are His children! How many of us of a former generation maybe recall the jingle that most of us were taught as little children which ran 'Said the sparrow to the Robin I should really like to know why these anxious human beings rush about and worry so. Said the Robin to the

Sparrow, I think that it must be that they have no Heavenly Father such as cares for you and me.' When our Lord in the Sermon on the Mount was dealing with the problem of worry, He set His teaching against the background of the Fatherhood of God! 'Your heavenly Father knoweth. . .'.

In our younger days we used to go on holiday by train. Our home was in Edinburgh and as the six of us set off we usually had added to us two or more cousins! There was a lot of luggage and as we had no car, we all had bicycles. We travelled to the Scottish Highlands, a favourite haunt of my Father. But to get there meant changing trains at Perth, changing from the old North British Railway to the Highland Railway whose engines all had exciting names! They were all called after the Rivers, the Lochs, the Bens, and biggest of all after the Clans! What a job it was transferring all the luggage and all the bicycles from the one platform to the other. But who do you think did all the worrying, all the caring? It was not the children, it was my Father! He saw to it all, though of course we all helped.

I feel sometimes that too many of us who call ourselves Christians and who have been born again into the family of God, have forgotten that we have a Father and that we are His children, 'Leave it all quietly *to God*, my soul,' remembering the Person He is and the People we are.

At the Keswick Convention there is a hymn that many of us associate with the meetings in the tent there, the first line reads, 'Like a river glorious is God's perfect peace. . .' The chorus reads,

'Stayed upon Jehovah, hearts are fully blessed,
Finding as He promised, *perfect peace and rest!*'

It is the hearts that are stayed upon Jehovah, and that have the right to be stayed upon Him, because we are His children, born again into His family by His Spirit, who find perfect peace and rest. What a pearl this verse is, what an insight it gives into what it means in practical down-to-earth terms, to trust in God. Let us then remember the Wholeness with which our Faith is asked to Trust, The Stillness in which our Faith is asked to Rest and the Fulness on which our Faith is asked to Count. 'Leave it all quietly to God my soul.'

How faith faces the future
'The Lord is my shepherd.' Psalm 23

One of the wonderful things about the Bible is that again and again one experiences the fact that reading a passage that is very, very familiar, for the thousandth time, one suddenly discovers truths that one had never seen before. So it was that on one occasion I was reading this very, very familiar psalm and suddenly noticed that David makes three future tense affirmations in the psalm. When I thought these through it seemed to me that they reveal how faith can face the future.

This psalm has been called the 'Pearl of Psalms'. Some commentators will differ in their interpretation of it. Some indeed see this not as just the Shepherd psalm but see David viewing his relationship with his Lord from different aspects. Dr Graham Scroggie sums it up like this, that here we see David speaking of the sheep and the shepherd, then the guide and the traveller, and finally the host and the banquet. Dr Alexander McLaren follows a similar line. But those of us who have read the little booklet called 'The Song of our Syrian Guest' in which the psalm is interpreted as seen through the eyes of an Eastern shepherd, realise that the Psalm is indeed of one piece throughout. It is indeed the shepherd Psalm.

We need to note the relationship on which the whole Psalm rests. David says 'The *Lord* is *my* shepherd' as if to say 'I don't know who the shepherd is who is looking after your life but *the Lord* is my shepherd, He is the one looking after my life.' He is indeed the good shepherd who gave his life for the sheep. At the heart of this psalm then lies this basic truth, the truth of belonging to someone. That someone is, of course, the Good Shepherd himself. This relationship has been very beautifully expressed in a hymn that we have often sung

at my mid-week Bible study when I was minister of St
George's Tron Church in Glasgow. I wonder if you know
it. This is how it goes:

Jesus my Lord will love me for ever
From him no power of evil will sever.
He gave his life to ransom my soul,
Now I belong to Him.

Chorus: Now I belong to Jesus, Jesus belongs to me
        Not for the years of time alone but for
        eternity.

Just as the sheep belongs to the shepherd so I belong to
Jesus. I recall once getting a letter in response to a
broadcast. It was rather a sad letter in which the writer
wrote 'I feel I belong to no one!' No Christian should
ever say that!

Someone has said very beautifully that 'whenever you
see a sheep, however desolate the moorland, windswept
and rain-washed it may be, you know that somewhere
there is a shepherd who owns the sheep. The sheep does
not own the shepherd, it is the other way round, the
shepherd owns the sheep.' So David says, 'The Lord is
my shepherd'. I remember this mutual relationship of
belonging being brought out in a very lovely way. I was
sitting in the audience of a convention in Dublin many
years ago. The preacher was the late Rev. George Mann,
rector of the Parish of Knocknamuckly. Both the name
of the rector and the parish have remained vividly in my
mind. He told the story of a minister, I wondered if it
was himself, who woke on a Monday morning feeling
very down. Sunday had not gone well and as Monday
was his day off he was in no hurry to get up out of bed.
His wife had prepared breakfast and breakfast was ready
so she told her two daughters to run upstairs to tell her
husband that it was time to come down. They ran to do
her bidding, the older one with the longer legs got there
first and running into the bedroom she flung herself on
the bed and threw her arms around her father. When
her little sister came in a moment or two later she gloated

over her little sister, saying 'I've got all there is of Daddy!' Of course that broke the little one's heart. She started crying and ran round to the other side of the bed and climbed up on to the bed and Daddy put out his arm and enfolded the little girl within his embrace. When her sobs ceased she looked over her Daddy's body at her bigger sister on the other side and said 'You've got all that there is of Daddy, but Daddy's got all that there is of me!'

What a delightful picture that is, we have all that there is of Christ but Christ has all that there is of us! And so the basic relationship and the basic truth and thought in this shepherd Psalm is the thought of belonging to Him who is the Good Shepherd. What then are the three affirmations that faith can make as faith faces the future?

The first affirmation is contained in the first three verses and begins with the words 'The Lord is my shepherd, *I shall not want.*' So faith faces the future and:

A life in which there is to be no lack.

There is going to be a sufficiency to meet life's daily needs and these are brought out in these first three verses. In one of our hymn versions of this Psalm, sung so often at weddings, it is put like this:

The King of love my shepherd is, whose goodness faileth never,
I nothing lack if I am His and He is mine for ever.'

Two things are held in view here. First of all we have (a) *a supplying of the needs of the sheep* and the needs are two-fold, first that they should be *fed* and so be strong and healthy and also that they should be *led* and so be safe. And the responsibility for both the feeding and leading of the sheep is the shepherd's and not the sheep's. So we read 'He maketh me to lie down in green pastures. He leadeth me beside still waters.' Of what does the feeding speak save what we call sometimes the means of grace. God has provided us with the Scriptures of truth, the privilege of prayer, the ministry of the

Spirit, the fellowship of the redeemed and all the fulness of His grace in Christ! Here there is to be found the enrichment, the encouragement, the equipment and the enablement that we need. But the sheep not only need to be fed, they need to be led.

And so here too we find the leading of the sheep and there are both negative and positive aspects of this. The Psalmist says that 'He restoreth my soul.' That word restore in the Hebrew means to 'turn back', to bring back, to restrain. The shepherd is recalling the sheep that would stray on to the land of another shepherd who would then have the right to possess the trespasser! I *think* this is what lies behind the words in Isaiah 30:21. Do you remember how the prophet says 'Thine ear shall hear a word behind thee, saying "This is the way, walk ye in it," *when* ye turn to the right hand and when ye turn to the left'! I used to think that that meant that when we came to a divide, a fork in the road, we would be told whether to go to the right or to the left! But now I think it means this, that if we do go to the right or we do go to the left, and that is the wrong way, then we will hear a voice saying 'Hey there! What are you doing? *This* is the way, walk ye in it.' So there is a sense in which God will never let us take the wrong turning without warning us that it is the wrong turning. So there is a negative aspect to the leading of the sheep.

But, supremely, there are positive aspects. 'He leadeth me in the paths of righteousness.' I believe the South African version speaks of 'the sheeptracks of righteousness', those bewildering sheeptracks that criss-cross the slopes of our lowland hills and pasture lands. What a wonderful truth it is that those who belong to the shepherd will be guided. The psalmist tells us in Psalm 25:9 'The meek will he guide in judgment.' Our Lord in his chapter on the good shepherd, John's gospel chapter 10, says 'When the good shepherd puts forth his sheep He goeth before them' and Paul writing in Romans 8:14 assures us that 'As many as are led by the Spirit of God, they are the sons of God.' So both the feeding of the flock and the leading of the flock are going to be part of our experience. These are the needs of the sheep.

But there is another thing involved and that is (b) *a safeguarding of the name of the shepherd*. It is all for 'His name's sake'. The condition of the sheep reflects at once on the good name of the shepherd and God's good name is at stake here. If the sheep are not fed, if the sheep are not led, the blame falls on the shepherd not on the sheep. I remember a delightful story told about some people who were on holiday at the seaside. As they walked along the road to go down to the beach they passed a shoeshine boy waiting to polish the shoes of those on holiday. He had such a winsome smile and attractive manner that when he asked if he could shine their shoes they agreed. After he had done his work they went on down to the beach. Now you can't walk along a beach without getting your shoes dirty and when they came back, of course, their shoes were covered with sand. They passed the small boy again and, as a good professional, he was looking at their feet and saw their dirty shoes and cried out 'Oh, please, may I shine your shoes?' They said, 'But you've already done it.' He replied, 'I don't want money this time,' he said, *but I can't have my work walking about looking like that*!' Can God afford to have us walking about living lives that are below par, getting into all kinds of muddles and mistakes? No, he can't! So the leading and the feeding of the sheep involve a safeguarding of the name of the shepherd. So faith faces the future and affirms that the future will hold a life in which there is to be no lack.

But this pearl of Psalms contains another confident 'I will'. In verses 4 and 5 David affirms 'I will fear no evil'. So as faith faces the future it is thinking of:

A life in which there is to be no fear!

No fear! 'Yea though I walk through the valley of the shadow of death I will fear no evil for thou art with me.' I want us to note (a) *how fearful we can be*. These verses speak of *places* in which we can be afraid, in v4, and of *forces* of which we can be afraid, in v5. Places in which we can be afraid! We read of '*the valley of the shadow of death*'. The NEB speaks of 'valleys as dark as death!'

We normally take this as referring to death itself and most certainly it includes death, but surely it has a much wider application. The shepherd may at any time lead the sheep through dark and gloomy ravines. He leads them through as he leads them from one pasture to another. Sometimes, sooner or later, most of us will pass through valleys like that, when the sun seems to vanish from our sky and the light seems to die out of our souls. This could be a dark valley of suffering, of ill-health, of loneliness, of old age or even of death itself.

Yes, there are places in which we can be afraid. But also there are *forces* of which we can be afraid, v5, 'Thou preparest a table before me *in the presence of mine enemies.*' The Eastern shepherd in that lovely commentary, 'The Song of our Syrian Guest' speaks of the vigilance that is called for from the shepherd lest there should be poisonous plants which, if eaten by the sheep would hurt them, lest there should be a viper's nest, lest there should be lurking beasts, wolves or lions. So the shepherd is aware of the enemies and so, too, are the sheep. There are forces that are dangerous, spiritual forces, human forces. They are dangerous because they could *deceive*. Our Lord, in John 8:44, calls the devil the father of lies, a liar! He is called the one who deceives the whole world. In any war we are told that truth is the first casualty and in the spiritual warfare it is true also!

There are forces that would *destroy*. Our Lord calls the devil a murderer. Peter in his first epistle speaks of the devil as being like a roaring lion. Of course he cannot destroy our salvation but he can destroy a great deal. He can destroy our peace, our joy, our usefulness, our witness. Yes, there are forces, indeed there is a trinity, of evil. It's called the world, the flesh and the devil. Bishop Taylor Smith used to define that trinity of evil as 'the world with all its allurements, the flesh with all its subtlety, the devil with all his experience!' We are right to be fearful of forces like that. How fearful we can be!

But we need not be fearful because here we read (b) *how faithful he will prove.* 'I will fear no evil *for Thou art with me*; Thou preparest a table before me in the presence of mine enemies.' The great fact which stills our fears is the fact that we are never alone. 'Lo, I am with you always', said Jesus and that *means* always. I love some of the old-fashioned hymns that are seldom sung now, I suppose the poetry is not good but there is nothing wrong with the theology and the tunes may not be good but they are singable! I wonder how many of us remember that old hymn with its great chorus,

'Fear not I am with thee, blessed golden ray,
Like a star of glory, lighting up my way.
Through the clouds of midnight, this bright promise shone,
I will never leave thee, never will leave thee alone.
No, never alone, no never alone,
He promised never to leave me, never to leave me alone.'

What a difference it makes if we are not alone in a place that's dangerous, facing forces that are too strong for us.

I remember very vividly an incident in my boyhood when I was about 12 or 13 and suffering from a very nasty boil or abcess. My mother, who was a trained nurse, did her best to cure it but she couldn't and my temperature was going up and up and up. I was confined to bed. One day the door of my bedroom opened and in came our family doctor. He was just as much a friend of the family as our doctor, but what startled me was that he didn't come alone, he came with his partner! I wondered what that meant. After he examined my boil (and it meant that I couldn't sit down, so you know where it was) he turned to his partner and said 'Do you think this will need an anaesthetic?' That really scared me, what were they going to do? They decided it didn't need an anaesthetic, a decision that I think they regretted and I certainly did! He then took out of his black bag one of the most wicked looking little knives I have ever seen. It glinted, and the blade was triangular, it was sharp and I knew he was going to use it! Just as my fears were reaching their maximum the door opened again and in came my dad. He slipped down on his knees beside me on the other side of the bed and held my hand. I have never forgotten that! What a difference it made not to be alone! And this of course is so true of the Christian, never alone! So when faith faces the future in which there is to be no lack, there is to be no fear.

Then we come to the final future tense affirmation in the last verse, v6. It reads 'Surely goodness and mercy shall follow me all the days of my life and I will die.' No, NO! '*and I will dwell in the house of the Lord for ever.*' Here is the third most amazing affirmation of faith. A future in which there is to be no lack, in which there is to be no fear, in which there is to be no death.

A life in which there is to be no death

So it does not say 'surely goodness and mercy will follow me all the days of my life and then I will die' but 'and then I will dwell in the house of the Lord for ever.' Here we have the picture of the flock safely folded at the end of the day. If we take days as being symbolical of our span of life here on earth there will come the time when our days on earth may end but not our life! What tremendous statements we find in our Bibles about this. In John 11:25, Jesus says 'Whosoever liveth and believeth in me shall never die.' In 2 Timothy 1:10, Paul writes of Jesus who 'hath abolished death and hath brought immortality and life to light through the gospel.' What then will the future hold? Two things here, first (*a*) *the unfailing goodness of God*. 'Surely goodness and mercy shall follow me *all* the days of my life', the days of my childhood, my youth, middle age, increasing age, old age and right through to the end, all the days, goodness and mercy! God's goodness, yes, we can be quite sure of that for God loves us and nothing will be allowed in our lives that is not permitted or planned by perfect love! Also God's mercy. We'll never get beyond the need of that, indeed the greater the saint the greater the sense of unworthiness. John McNeil the great Scottish preacher called 'goodness and mercy' God's two collie dogs. If ever you have seen a shepherd at work with his dogs you know how those dogs keep continually circling round the sheep. God's goodness and God's mercy.

But not only the unfailing goodness of God but also (b) *the unfolding glory of home.* 'I will dwell in the house of the Lord forever'. We are not told much about heaven but we are told by Christ that it has been prepared by Him, 'I go to prepare a place for you'! What expectations that will arouse! When human love plans and purposes for those it loves how confident, how expectant love is that everything will be just right. That reminds me of a lady in my church in Glasgow, I think her name was Mrs Grant. It was a delight to visit her. If she had managed to get to church which she did whenever she could, and I called later that week, she would say to me 'Well Mr Duncan, I was at church on Sunday and it was *just wonderful*!' At harvest time we loved to send gifts of fruit and flowers and vegetables round to the widows and the elderly. The young people did that after the evening service. If I called the following week just to see if the young folks had done their duty and called to see Mrs Grant, she would greet me with 'Oh, Mr Duncan, the young people came. Look what they brought, isn't it *just wonderful*!' At Christmas time we loved just to give a little extra to some of the widows and the old folk to help them. I would slip an envelope with a Christmas card and something in it and leave it on the mantelpiece just as I was leaving. Mrs Grant would thank me and she would say, 'Oh, Mr Duncan, that's very kind of you. You're *just wonderful*!' Then the time came and Mrs Grant slipped away Home! I took the funeral and I said to the relatives 'I am quite certain that as soon as your mother opened her eyes on the other side, she would look around and say, 'Oh, isn't it *just wonderful*!' And it will be!

I have a lovely memory of my fellowship with Dr Paul Rees who told how on one occasion he was summoned home in a great hurry. His father was slipping away. He got back just in time. His father was nearly at the end of the road, well down the valley. Paul said he had to bend low to hear what his father was saying. This is what his father said, 'Paul, I'm nearly Home!' And that's what its going to be. No lack, no fear, no death, when you and I can say 'the Lord is my shepherd.' Can you say that? I hope you can. I wonder if you know that verse from a lovely hymn which goes like this, and I end with it:

Let me no more my comfort draw from my frail hold on thee,
But only in this rejoice with awe, Thy mighty grasp on me!
No lack! No fear! No death!

5: 'He is Lord' . . . but is He Lord?

I wonder how many people who have received a set of silver coffee spoons or teaspoons, after the first moments in which they have admired the gift, maybe received at the time of their wedding, have then turned the spoons over to look for something? They have been looking to see if the spoons are solid silver or just silver plated. What they have been looking for is the hallmark as it is called. In Britain that hallmark which is only put on to goods made of solid silver is the mark of a tiny little lion. If the hallmark is there, they, not surprisingly, are even more delighted and grateful for the gift. Those spoons are solid silver. What would you say is the hallmark of a valid Christian life, a life being lived as God wants it to be? Some would say at once, the hallmark is 'love'. The fruit of the Spirit says Paul is 'love'. But wait a minute! What is the hallmark of love? Well let us take Jesus for our authority on that point, He said that 'He that hath my commandments and keepeth them, he it is that loveth Me.' So the hallmark of true love is 'obedience'. Somewhere else in this book we will be looking and examining the true nature of Christian love in more detail. It is a word in very common use in many Christian circles today, but I sometimes wonder if half of those talking about love and singing about it, have a clue as to its real nature! But let us come back to the hallmark of love, it is, so says Jesus, obedience. When I first went to the Keswick Convention, not as a speaker, but as a Scoutmaster camping with a troop of Scouts belonging to my father's Church, (my father was incidentally speaking at Keswick that year) I had attended all the meetings and had enjoyed them, but nothing of any particular significance had come through to me! The convention in those pre-war days went on over the second weekend when a testimony meeting was held on the Sunday afternoon. On the Saturday I was stopped by the then secretary of the convention, the late Mr J. M. Waite! 'I want you to speak at the testimony meeting tomorrow,' he said. Apart from being petrified at the thought, I was not sure if I had a testimony to give about any special blessing I had received. On the Sunday morning I went to worship in the Methodist Church in Southey Street where the preacher was an anglican, Canon St John Thorpe, he preached on 'Five Whatso-evers of the Christian Life.' The first was God's word to me, 'Whatsoever He saith unto you, do it!' There and then I faced the challenge of the Lordship of Christ, there I learned that the hallmark of the true Christian is found in his obedience to His Lord. The two messages which follow underscore that truth, a truth which badly needs to be learned and applied today. One of the love-liest of all the modern choruses begins with the words, 'He is Lord, He is risen from the dead and He is Lord.' The tune is beautiful. But as I listen, I sometimes find myself asking 'how many people are singing a lie to God' 'He is Lord' they are singing, but is He?

Love's glad servitude

'*I love my master . . . I will not go out free.*' Exodus 21:5

When the late Mr Fred Mitchell spoke on these words at the Keswick Convention in England a number of years ago, he chose as a title for his address 'Love's consecration of all for ever.' These are wonderful words and they conjure up a wonderful picture of a New Testa-ment relationship portrayed in the regulations of the Old Testament days. There was no word that St Paul and the other apostles were more fond of to describe their relationship to their Lord, than that they were 'the slaves' or 'the servants' of Jesus Christ. Paul uses this, Peter uses it, James uses it and Jude. In passing and by way of introduction, may we note that while slavery would seem to have been permitted in Israel in those far-off days, it was alleviated and mitigated by this fact, that a limit was set to its duration. 'Six years he shall serve, and in the seventh he shall go out free for nothing.' So at the end of six years the slave was promised liberty! But if the slave so desired it, he could continue in the service of his Master for ever! The regulations stated it in these words 'But if the servant shall plainly say, "I love my master, I will not go out free." he shall serve him for ever'. Love's glad servitude, love's consecration of all for ever.

I suggest that, first, we have here in the Old Testament pattern a reminder of:

The motive of love's consecration

'I love my master.' Think for a moment of (*a*) *the revelation that the years would bring.* 'Six years he shall serve.' What an insight those years of service would bring to the slave, what intimate knowledge and understanding of the nature and character of his master. In John 2:1–11 we have the account of the first miracle, the changing of the water into wine at Cana of Galilee. Tucked away in that incident we have a suggestive phrase, 'the servants knew.' That indeed makes a theme does it not for another sermon? The insights of service! There was much that the servants knew about the miracle, that no-one else knew. There is much that any servants would know about their master that no-one else would know. Indeed there would not be much that a servant would not know about a house, or a family, about the children, about the mistress, or about the master.

Often the insights of the servants would be very different from those of the more casual observer. We have all had the experience of walking through a beautifully decorated, carpeted and furnished show room of a great store! Then perhaps we go past the door that is marked 'Staff only', and as we pass the door swings open, and we get one brief glimpse into the precincts beyond. We see no carpet on the floor there, no panelling of the walls in choice wood, but rather tiled walls and stone steps going to the lower regions perhaps! No, there is not much that slaves would not know about their master. But here the Word of God allows the possibility that a slave might have such a wonderful master that at the end of six years of intimate knowledge, the slave has been driven to this one conclusion expressed in these words, 'I love my master.'

Some slaves would not be able to say this. Those six years of service could breed only hate and fear. The day of release from harshness and cruelty would be longed for and would be eagerly grasped. But for a few others it would be different. To know some masters would be to love them, and those six years would reveal only utter worthiness, utter goodness, unfailing kindness and care, and the slave would have to confess 'I love my master.'

I want to suggest that this knowledge is in the plan of God for us, in our relationship with our Master. We are to know him. Listen to some of the scriptures which underscore this pattern of the divine intention: 'He that loveth me shall be loved of my Father, and I will love him, and I will manifest myself to him'; 'This I pray, that your love may abound yet more and more in knowledge'; and St Paul's great ambition as a Christian 'that I may know him. . .'. The slave would know his master, so the Christian will know his Lord! I wonder if we know him? Can we say with the slave of Old Testament times 'I love my master'? What a Master we have in Christ! So we have noted the revelation the years would bring.

Then we must note (b) *the response the heart would make*. The motive of love's consecration is love itself. So consecration, surrender and obedience, have nothing to do with an arbitrary demand from the rule of a tyrant. Rather they have to do with a glad response, offered willingly from within. And note that the New Testament experience adds something not found in the Old Testament parable. We all know that 'the gift of God is eternal life through Jesus Christ', and that by the acceptance of that life we become children of God. But I hope we all also know that besides the gift being a gift of a new life it is the gift of a new love! 'The love of God *has been shed* abroad in our hearts by the Holy Ghost given to us', so writes Paul in Romans 5:5. We cannot divorce the life in Christ from the love that is in Christ. Note carefully what Paul says, it is '*the love of God*' not, as some theologians would maintain, our knowledge of the love of God!

This is not a love that we have to work up, it is a love we have to let out. It is there already within, and our experience bears witness to this. Before we became Christians we did not love, we did not value the things of God. We did not love the house of God, the Word of God, the Lord's Day, the Lord's will, the Lord's people. After we were converted and became Christians, we found to our amazement that all that was changed. All these things which before had held no interest for us, suddenly became important. John says in 1 John 3:14 that this is the evidence of the new life within. 'We know that we have passed from death unto life, *because we love. . . .*' And so with the life came the love, with the new life came the new love, the love of God boomeranging back as it were and becoming a love for God. This is not simply something that God requires, it is something that he bestows and creates within us by His Spirit. So in the fellowship that we have in Christ down the passing years, we so come to know him that he becomes to us the chiefest among ten thousand and the altogether lovely one. So here we have the motive of love's consecration in four simple words 'I love my master'.

Secondly we have here what I have ventured to call:

The meaning of love's consecration

'He shall serve him for ever.' This slave was to be left in no doubt as to the magnitude of the issues involved in the choice confronting him. I think this meant at least two things, firstly (*a*) *the acceptance of a new authority*, 'he shall serve him.' The whole ordering of the slave's life was now going to pass into other hands. A slave possessed nothing, decided nothing. He was simply there

82

to be utterly available, to be at the disposal, the beck and call of his master, to do or not to do, to go or not to go, for any task or no task.

How vastly different this pattern of living would be from that of other men. Let us note that this too is the New Testament pattern. Paul writes 'ye are not your own for ye are bought with a price'! Again in Ephesians 2 Paul describes the basic pattern for those who are now Christians. He reminds the Ephesians that before they were in Christ, the whole pattern of their life was quite different. Two principles dominated their conduct, either they did what others did: 'ye walked according to the course of this world' (v1), or you did what you wanted to do, 'fulfilling the desires of the flesh and of the mind' (v3). Now these are the principles upon which the unconverted man lives. He does what others do, he does what he wants! But a slave was not free to live on either of these patterns. He certainly did not necessarily do what he wanted, nor did he do what others did. He did one thing only, and that was what his master wanted him to do. To St. Paul in the very hour of his conversion on the Damascus road the understanding of this other way of life had come, when he said, 'Lord what wilt *Thou* have me to do?'

Now this is momentous, this is tremendous! But I believe that this is basic and I believe that revival in the Church tarries for this one reason, and one reason only — that Christians are not prepared to recognise the new authority under which they must live. What we do with the time we are given is not for us to decide. What we do with the money we have, is not for us to decide. What we are going to do with the life that we plan to live, is not for us to decide. What we are going to do with the gifts we have, is not for us to decide. What we are going to do with the home we build, is not for us to decide!

I feel that the relationship of so many Christians to their Master is more like that of a flirt rather than a lover. A flirt is somebody who wants all the excitement of love, without the responsibilities, someone who wants all the gifts without the relationship — the kind of girl who will go out with a boy just for the sake of the boxes of chocolates that he is going to give her. She has no intention of marrying him. Is it possible that many of us are just flirting with Christ? We want the fun and the pleasure, the comfort and excitement of being a Christian, but we don't want to enter into this relationship of complete obedience and union with him.

Why are our mission stations understaffed? Why are they ill-equipped. Why is it that Christian literature is just a trickle instead of a flood? Why is it that our churches are empty? Why is it that our Bible study groups are ill attended? Why is it that our prayer meetings are so small? Why is it that we lack choir members in our churches? Why is it that we lack Sunday school teachers? Is it because too many Christians are running their own lives to suit themselves? But a slave does not do that, a slave has absolutely nothing belonging to himself, not a thing.

We have noted the acceptance of a new authority for any task. We need also to note (*b*) *the permanence of that new authority*: 'ye shall serve him *for ever*' for any task, and for all time! How decisive and determinative this choice can be! What a choice to make! I wonder if we might be tempted to say 'This is far too big a matter, you are setting the standard far too high! This is not a thing that I could do.' Maybe I am speaking to somebody who is young, and among the plans which you have for the coming days is your plan to marry. In the marriage service you will most likely be asked this question, 'Are you willing to forsake all others and keep thee only unto him, to her, *so long as ye both shall live*?' So that is the relationship of love that is intended to be for all time, is it not? We do not grudge it. We do not rebel against it. Of course not! The reason is because we love, that is all!

I believe that as in human relationship between husband and wife there is a place for the reaching of such a decision, so in Scripture and in Christian experience there is a place for such a choice. There is a place for consecration and a surrender so full and so complete that in one sense it will never have to be repeated, although the implications of it will go on being discovered and worked out. Here then is the New Testament authority for just such a thing. In Romans 6:13 Paul writes 'Yield yourselves unto God as those that are alive from the dead and your members as instruments of righteousness unto God' and the force of that word yield is 'once and for all'. I maintain that there is nothing tyrannous about this but love would just not have it any other way. So the hymn writer agrees and says '*In full and glad* surrender I give myself to thee, thine utterly and only and evermore to be.' So I want us to notice that the hymn writer says that it is *in full and glad surrender*, so there is an acceptance and a permanence about the new authority under which my life is to pass.

Finally we find in this Old Testament parable of New Testament truth what I have called:

The moment of love's consecration

And here it is very deliberate. In vv5 & 6 we read 'If the servant shall plainly say, 'I love my master . . . I will not go out free. . .' then his master shall bring him unto the judges, he shall also bring him to the door, or to the doorpost, and his master shall bore his ear through with an awl, and he shall serve him for ever.' The first thought which comes to me is to notice that this decision was (*a*) *to be reached personally*. '*If the servant shall plainly say* "I love my master. . ." '. The Scripture does not say 'If the master says'. No doubt during those six years there might well have been moments when the freedom of others seemed attractive, it had its appeal and sometimes too with the Christian looking out upon the worldling living without the restraints and responsibilities the Christian may have, such freedom might seem attractive. There was, if he so chose, no need to go on serving his master. It was not the master's place, it was not the place of any other servant, it is not my place to reach this decision for you but if *you* shall plainly say 'I love my master', that is enough. It was to be reached personally.

It was also (*b*) *to be revealed publicly*. He was to be brought to the judges or to the door, there was to be nothing secretive about this. It was to be done frankly, openly and publicly and his ear was to be pierced through with an awl. So he would bear the mark of a slave publicly wherever he went. This does sometimes happen in a meeting for Christians or a great evangelistic crusade but that is not the main thought. This is something that will show itself in the office, the hospital ward, the home, the school, as a doctor, as a minister, as a missionary, as a business man or as a housewife — the fact that the Christian is serving Christ and serving him for ever just cannot be concealed. Every day, everywhere, the bond slave of Jesus Christ is marked out as being distinctively different, in his standards, his ambitions, his motives, his resources, his whole programme, and the reason is that there has come a day in his life when he confronted the choice that every Christian faces and has said 'I love my master, I will not go out free'. May I end by recording a memory from my younger days, of a lady, the widow of the late Rev. Gordon Watt, a speaker at the Keswick Convention. The thing that intrigued me as a young Christian was the brooch she wore. It was in gold, and it spelt out just one word — 'Rabboni.' Master! 'I love my master, I will not go out free.' Will we dare to say that if we have never said it before? Do we want to say it? Will we say it and say it now and go out and 'serve him for ever'?

The must of submission
'And it came to pass, when Joshua was by Jericho, that he lifted up his eyes and behold . . . a man'. Joshua 5:13–6:5

It sometimes happens that in one's study of the Word of God there comes a time when a lesson learned is peculiarly urgent and vital in a given situation. So it was when not so long ago I was re-reading this familiar incident of Joshua before Jericho. At that time I and others with me were facing the massive task, or so it seemed to me, of ministering yet once again to the great crowds at the Keswick Convention with the vast needs represented there and the vast issues lying beyond the crowds. Like Joshua I was surveying the massive walls of my Jericho when as I looked at the experience of Joshua on that occasion, I learned some lessons that seemed to me then and now of urgent relevance and importance in the life of the Church. I want to share them with you as it may well be that not a few of us are facing some Jericho in our lives and we badly need to learn the lessons to be found here.

If life is for most of us a battle then we might well title our theme for today 'Briefing for Battle', or 'The Must of Submission'. I want us to note:

The re-assessment of Joshua's task

Joshua 5:13: 'And it came to pass, when Joshua was by Jericho that he lifted up his eyes and behold . . . a man'. Here we must note: (a) *The Problem that Concerned Joshua*. 'When Joshua was by Jericho' his problem could be summed up in one word, 'Jericho', and is it not true that very often in life your problem or mine might well be summed up as briefly as Joshua's was, in one word. The scene is not a difficult one to imagine. The mighty fortress of Jericho blocked and barred the way to any further advance by Joshua and the chosen people. There the city stood with its massive defences and armed garrison and behind the city the Judean hills rose steeply. It was right and reasonable that time and thought should be given to surveying the city, for if God's destiny for Israel was to be realised then this difficulty must be resolved. And so in the dawn light Joshua went out no doubt to reconnoitre the ground. For him Jericho was the problem that concerned him.

But Joshua is not the only one with problems in his life. How true it is both of individual Christians and of local congregations and indeed of the universal Church that we know what it is to face problems that seem to defy all solution. We recognise that God has a destiny both for the individual Christian and for the corporate life of the Church and yet so often some massive problem seems to block the way and makes advance difficult if not impossible. In our personal life, in our congregational life, or at times on a wider front, still Christians are found surveying the scene and spending much time and thought assessing the strength of the Jericho garrison, measuring the height and thickness of the Jericho walls, planning, hoping, wondering, fearing, facing the problem that at that particular moment is the concern of that particular Christian or congregation. 'When Joshua was by Jericho' I wonder if someone at this very moment is conscious supremely of some problem that concerns them deeply in their spiritual experience. But notice how we read, 'When Joshua was by Jericho, that he lifted up his eyes and behold' — not Jericho — 'behold a man', and so we find here not simply the problem that concerned Joshua but: (b) *The Person that Confronted Joshua*. It was this thought that gripped me. Joshua went out to look at Jericho and found instead that he was looking at Jesus. That is why I have suggested that the first principle that we can learn and need to learn, and must learn, from this incident of long ago centres round the re-assessment of Joshua's task. Joshua thought that his task primarily was concerned with Jericho but he learned that his first task was concerned with Jesus; for I believe that this was one of the several pre-incarnation appearances of the Lord recorded in the Old Testament scriptures. It would certainly seem to be so from the words of the speaker and the attitude of Joshua the listener.

If we wish to call witnesses to support this view listen to the voice of the great Dr. Whyte of Free St. George's, Edinburgh, 'All down sacred history through Israel, and not less through England and Scotland, there have never failed prophets to preach how to war a good warfare nor has the Lord's host lacked leaders like Joshua who fell *at that divine Captain's feet* and worshipped.' 'That divine Captain', the Captain of our salvation, so Dr. Whyte would seem to believe that this was none other than the person of Jesus Christ! Listen again to another distinguished preacher from the city of Edinburgh, Dr. Graham Scroggie of Charlotte Chapel, Edinburgh, '*God in Christ appears in many aspects to His people* and always in the manner most suited to the circumstances and need of the hour; to Jacob He came as a wrestler, to Moses He appeared in a flame of fire, *to Joshua He reveals Himself as a warrior*, to the afflicted He is the God of comfort, to the depressed He is the God of hope, to the lonely He is a friend, to the storm-tossed He is an anchor and to the longing soul He is the Lord who meets our every need.' 'To Joshua He reveals Himself as a warrior.' And so with these two distinguished witnesses to support our own personal conviction that this was a pre-incarnation appearance of the Lord we would reiterate the truth that Joshua had to learn that his initial problem was not concerned with Jericho but was concerned with Jesus, 'When Joshua was by Jericho he lifted up his eyes and behold' — not Jericho — 'behold a man'. In other words the Lord was in effect saying 'your first task Joshua is not with Jericho, it is with me.' The re-assessment of his task!

I believe that nothing is more urgently true than this, that whether it be the individual Christian or the local congregation, or the denominational or universal Church, the first task of the Church is with her Lord and with His Lord-ship. I note two things stressed here — first of all *the importance of the coming of Christ*, 'Am I now come', and the second thing that is stressed here is *the insistence on the control of Christ* '*As Captain* am I now come.' Joshua seems to have realised this with his own response, 'What saith my Lord unto *his servant*?' This was Joshua's recognition of the divine presence. How similar his words are to the words of St. Paul when as Saul of Tarsus he was confronted by the risen Christ on the road to Damascus, 'Lord, what wilt Thou have me to do?' Not only was Christ there but it was recognised that He must be in control. Oh, if only the Church, if only the individual Christian, if only you and I could make this re-assessment of our task what new hope might we find! Our first business is with our Lord. I remember reading many years ago of a Christian soldier who used to say that he recognised that his first duty, every day, was to stand before his Lord, his Captain and then to stand behind Him. The re-assessment of Joshua's task.

I want us to note secondly:

The readjustment in Joshua's life

'What saith my Lord unto his servant?' These were the words of Joshua. He might well have expected some word now about Jericho but not so, for in chapter 5 v15 we read, 'And the captain of the Lord's host said unto Joshua, loose thy shoe from off thy foot; for the place whereon thou standest is holy. And Joshua did so.' The re-assessment of his task first, and secondly the readjustment in his life. First of all Joshua had to deal with Jesus and then secondly the Lord had to deal with Joshua. There is not a word about Jericho yet. I want us to note:
(a) *The area of God's concern* God was not concerned about Jericho, not yet, but He was concerned about the life of His servant. It would seem as if there was something wrong with Joshua here. Had it been an oversight? Had it been a bit of carelessness? Was there a lack of humility betraying itself in Joshua's conduct? The rules governing man's conduct in God's presence had already been taught to Moses and no doubt had been passed on to Joshua but these rules had been broken. It was a small matter but God wanted to deal with that first. And so it was that when Joshua addressed his question 'What saith my Lord unto his servant?' and no doubt expected that the Captain of the Lord's host would have something to say about Jericho, to his utter amazement he found that the Captain had something to say about the servant!

How often this is the case in spiritual experience. We want God to deal with others and all the time God wants to deal with us! Do you remember how it happened in the life of Jacob, when Jacob was returning home, he got news that Esau was coming to meet him? We read of this in Genesis chapter 32. The fear of Esau brought Jacob to his knees; and so in loneliness he waits to pray, and no doubt in his praying he wanted God to deal with Esau! Esau was the man he feared, but he discovered in the solitude of that encounter that God wanted to deal *with Jacob* himself, and so we read 'There wrestled a man *with him* until the breaking of the day!' Jacob was unrepentant. He had never faced up to his own failure and God was determined that this should be brought to an end! And so it is we read in 1 Peter 4:17 'Judgment must begin at the house of God' So often we who are Christians want the world to be obedient that the truth of God and all the time we ourselves are not obedient to His will! 'What saith my Lord unto His servant?' And the Captain of the Lord's host said. . .' What would he say to you? Let us note then the area of God's concern was the life of His servant, Joshua. And note also: (*b*) *The assent to God's command* 'And Joshua did so' v15. It was as simple as that. But refusal here would have meant rejection. Is it because we refuse that God rejects? The whole Bible witnesses to the fact that before God uses a man God proves a man, and the point at which God seeks to prove us is in the area of our obedience. Do you remember how it was so in the life of Gideon? Before he became the overthrower of the enemy who oppressed his nation he had first of all to overthrow the altar of Baal in his own home! It was so in the life of Abraham, in Genesis 22:18. Blessing was to come to all the nations of the earth and the reason 'because thou hast obeyed my voice.' It was so in the life of Christ Himself, in Philippians chapter 2 vv8 and 9 we read, 'He became obedient unto death, even the death of the cross *wherefore* God also hath highly exalted him.' It was Charles Finney who said that revival consists in a new obedience; and the problem in the Church is not that we do not know the will of God but that we will not do it, and as a result the name of God is dishonoured in our lives, the Spirit of God is grieved, and the will of God is left undone. And so the re-assessment of his task was to be followed by the readjustment in his life, and then and only then did the Lord come to deal with Jericho. This was the order then — Jesus, Joshua, *and then* Jericho! that is still the order, the battle order, in all spiritual conflict. And so we learn the third lesson that Joshua had to learn:

Having dealt with matters in their correct order what will the Lord now have to say about Jericho? Let us note how: (*a*) *The Lord revealed His intentions of victory* chapter 6 v2: 'I have given into thine hand Jericho' God's intention was victory and triumph. The thought that startled and shook me was simply this, that what was a problem to Joshua was no problem at all to Jesus. What are God's intentions for the Christian? Surely they are the same. God's intention is victorious living. 'Sin shall not have dominion over you,' Romans 6:14. The witness of countless Christians has been 'I can do all things through Christ which strengtheneth me,' Philippians 4:13. Listen again to the testimony of St. Paul in Romans 8:37. 'In all these things we are more than conquerors through him that loved us'. If this is God's intention for the individual Christian, what is God's intention for the Church? Have you ever stopped to ponder over the words of our Lord in Matthew 16:18: 'The gates of hell shall not prevail against it.' In the very announcement of the birth of our Lord the message was declared 'thou shalt call his name Jesus, for he shall save his people from their sins.' God's purpose is one of victory and triumph, one of irresistible advance. From time to time in history it has been so. In certain lives it has been demonstrated that not only is this the purpose of God but that it is the pattern of life that a Christian can live. Let us remember then that God's intention is for victory but let us also note: (*b*) *God's instructions for victory* Strange instructions indeed they were. Was ever battle fought like this battle? Surely not. But God's ways are not our ways. It is 'not by might, nor by power, but by my Spirit saith the Lord'. There are just two things we want to note about the strategy of God that was communicated to Joshua. First of all — it was *shaped by God*. Oh that the Christian Church would learn to listen to God's voice and fight its battles in God's way! The New Testament speaks of the power of the Holy Spirit; it speaks of the weapon of all prayer; it speaks of the sword of the spirit which is the Word of God. The New

Testament reminds us that the weapons of our warfare are not carnal, they are not human or fleshly, they are spiritual weapons, for ultimately the conflict of the Christian is fought and won or lost in the realm of the spirit. But not only was the strategy for victory shaped by God it had to be *shared by all*. This is brought out again and again. The task was too great, and so it is still. Everybody was to be in the battle. This was not to be the work of the few but to be the work of all. And so it is with the conflict of the Christian Church today. So often so much is left by so many to so few, and that is not God's way. When we come to the New Testament we find that although the functions of every individual Christian may be as varied as the functions of the different members of the body, nevertheless every member has its function and so too every single Christian will count in the battle. And so it was that Joshua fought the battle of Jericho and we all know what history has to say about the result: 'And the walls came tumbling down'. But after all, it wasn't Joshua alone, it was Jesus in command and Joshua His obedient servant with the people of God behind him. May God grant that we too may know what it is to be briefed for battle by the same divine Captain of our salvation, and may we too know what it is to enter into His triumph and demonstrate His power to overcome and to deliver to the glory of His name, as we submit in obedience to His perfect Will!

6: Understanding the Holy Spirit's place in our lives

Someone once said that 'if the Devil can't stop a person being converted he will then see to it that they are diverted'. Now, that is a statement worth thinking over when we come to view the scene in the church today with reference to our understanding of the person and work of the Holy Spirit. In my own thinking quite a seemingly simple statement by a preacher at the Gulf Coast Keswick Convention held in Houston, Texas, gave the jolt to my thinking about the Holy Spirit that I needed. He was commenting in quite a casual way upon the last words of Christ to His Church about the Holy Spirit, words recorded in Acts 1:8, 'You shall receive power after that the Holy Ghost is come upon you and you shall be witnesses unto Me unto the uttermost parts of the earth.' The comment he made was to the effect that he hoped that we had noticed that the promise of the power of the Holy Spirit was linked up with the task of witnessing to the world. In other words that the Holy Spirit was not given to me so that I could have a wonderful time, but so that through me the Holy Spirit could do a wonderful job! Most of my thinking about the Holy Spirit had been slanted in the direction of what the Holy Spirit could do for me! Then as I began to read my Bible more carefully I realised how right the speaker was. Listen to what Christ said in the Temple, 'If any man thirst let him come unto Me and drink, he that believeth in Me, *out of* his inner being shall flow rivers of living water. This spake He of the Spirit who was not yet given because Jesus was not yet glorified.' The rivers were to *flow out* to others. Even 'the fruit of the Spirit' reminded me that the fruit of a tree exists *for others*. The gifts of the Spirit are for the 'edifying of the church'. So it was that when later on I was asked as President of the UCCF to give my presidential address at their annual conference at Swanick, the conference title being '^ Festival of the Holy Spirit', I dared to begin my address on Acts 1:8 by sharing the adjustment in my own thinking. I said that while I appreciated the title of the Conference, I wanted to suggest that the Holy Spirit was not given so that we could hold festivals, although festivals do have a place in the life of the Christian, the Holy Spirit was not given so that we could have a wonderful time but the Holy Spirit was given so that we could do a wonderful job. This shifting of the balance in our thinking is badly needed today. Memory takes me back to a dream of Miss Amy Wilson Carmichael, the great missionary to India, who said that one night she dreamt that she was watching a procession of Indians walking in single file one behind the other. When she looked closer she saw that they were blind. To her horror she saw that they were walking towards the edge of a precipice and one by one they fell to their deaths! Then she noticed a group of Christians sitting on the grass near to where the Indians fell, and they were *making daisy chains*! I wonder what Amy Wilson Carmichael's dream would be if she dreamt it today, what would the Christians be doing?

The release of the Spirit

'Work out your own salvation with fear and trembling.'
Philippians 2:12

'Work out your own salvation with fear and trembling, for God is at work in you both to will and to do of His good pleasure.' This is one of the great texts of the Bible. Of course Paul is not contradicting himself; it is not salvation in the sense of getting right with God to which he is referring. He says elsewhere, 'By the works of the flesh shall no man be justified.' I believe we could render our text a little more freely: 'Work out *your own experi-*

ence of God's saving grace. Work it out to its complete-
ness, with fear and trembling, for God is at work in both
to will and to do of His good pleasure.' So I want, if I
may, to share with you three aspects of the Christian
experience, lived out in that full sense, that seem to me
to be of very great importance and needing to be stressed,
and which are enshrined here! First of all we have to
take into account:

The variations in our lives of the purposes of God

Now it *may* be that what Paul is saying is, 'Now that
I'm not visibly with you, work it all out on your own.'
But it may also be that He is thinking more specifically
and individually and saying to the Philippians, 'Work
out your own experience of God's saving grace with fear
and trembling.' In other words, he is suggesting that the
pattern of God's purpose for each of our lives is not
necessarily intended to be the same; and that there is
infinite variety in God's working out, in the fullest sense,
our individual experiences of His saving grace!

It has been very well said that God never makes a
duplicate, always an original. He does not want 'copy-
cat Christians'. Even identical twins are not identical! I
actually married one. I sometimes wonder whether it
was the right one that turned up! They were so alike it
was very difficult to tell them apart — but even they
were *not* identical. I wonder if the words of a saintly old
Scottish minister, Fraser of Brea would ring a bell in
somebody's mind? He put it like this. 'My soul is not to
hang at any man's girdle.' A lot of Christians today
would do well to take that to heart. We are almost in
danger of becoming a Corinthian church today, when
human leadership is beginning to take over from the
control of the Spirit.

Encouragement for our hearts. I want to suggest that
these variations in our lives in the purposes of God bring
encouragement for our hearts. So often we face two kinds
of dangers in growing up into Christian maturity. The
first is the temptation to think we must be like some
other Christian! But I don't find in my Bible that we are

96

necessarily to try and be like other Christians! You can sometimes see this more visibly in Christians holding prominent positions. I hold Billy Graham in the highest possible regard — he has done a wonderful work. But after a visit to the UK from Billy Graham we tend to get a whole crop of imitation Billy Grahams — men who develop a slight American accent, and twist their Bibles the way Billy twists his when he's preaching! That's a lot of nonsense! God only made one Billy, and He doesn't want any more. He made you to be you, because He wanted you to be you, not anybody else!

I have also found among a lot of Free Church ministers a tendency to mould their ministry on that of the late Dr Martin Lloyd-Jones. The Doctor would preach for an hour, so they reckon they should preach for an hour! I tell them, 'If Dr Martin Lloyd-Jones did it, it would be unforgettable — if you do it, it will be unforgiveable!' And so you and I are tempted, especially when we are young, to look at other Christians, and say 'I could never be that . . . I could never do that. . .' Well, perhaps the Lord doesn't want you to!

The other temptation is of course to try to make other people like us, to force them into our mould. I met an old lady who'd been carrying a great burden for years, somebody who claimed to have received the gift of speaking in tongues had told this poor soul that if she couldn't speak in tongues she wasn't a Christian! Well, that too is a lot of nonsense! I believe there is a gift of tongues but like Paul I don't think it's an important one! I do think it is one of the gifts of the Spirit but I don't think I am meant to tell anybody what gift they should have! That would be to appropriate to myself a power and authority that belongs to the Holy Spirit alone, not to me!

God wants each one of us to be different. He has put us at the centre of what Dr Paul Rees calls 'expanding circles of contacts', and that is your area of opportunity. He has given you a personality that is unique, because He wants to use it. God can reach people through your personality that He could never reach through mine.

There is *enrichment for the church*. There's encourage-

ment here for our hearts. Also of course there's enrichment for the church. That's why Paul points out, in
1 Corinthians 11, that every Christian has a gift and the
Holy Spirit gives different gifts to different people,
because different gifts are needed in the work of the
church. He says, 'How ridiculous it would be if the
whole body were to be all made up of one member! Just
a huge nose! Or just a huge foot walking along!' That is
what Paul said, and I think he had a twinkle in his eye
when he said it! And yet there are some people who
seem to say that every Christian ought to have the same
gift! May I submit again, that's all a lot of nonsense!

Maybe you're a very good listener. You're no good at
talking, but you're a good listener — well, I tell you,
the world needs folk who listen just as much as it needs
folk who talk! You might be no use at all at preaching
a sermon, but you're very good at baking scones. God
can use scones! Do you look upon your home as somewhere where you can show God's caring love to people
and invite them in; not to talk to them about their souls,
but just to show God's caring concern and love for them
as people?

There is then a variation in our lives in the purposes
of God. We've got to be ready and willing to accept
ourselves. I wonder whether somebody needs to do that,
to accept the fact that you are different? Maybe you're
not married. Prepare to accept that until God changes
it, because there are things you can do that married
people can't.

Encouragement for our hearts, enrichment for the
church, and then to the main thrust — 'for God is at
work in you.' That speaks of:

The operation in our lives of the Spirit of God

'God is at *work in you*.' But is He? Is He?

I want to note first of all, *how the Holy Spirit can be
restrained* in our lives. My Bible makes this quite clear.
I know some people make much of what they call 'irresistible grace'; but it's not a phrase I find anywhere in
my Bible! Nor do I find anywhere that God's grace is

irresistible either to sinners or saints. As for sinners, I find Jesus grieving over Jerusalem saying 'How often would I and ye would not,' and I find Stephen challenging his accusers, 'You do always resist the Spirit of God' — nothing irresistible there! As for believers, I find Paul warning the believers, 'Grieve not the Holy Spirit.' Then I can grieve Him! I find Paul saying 'Quench not the Spirit.' Then I can quench Him! He says to Timothy, 'Neglect not the spirit! — so I can neglect the gift! There's nothing irresistible there! I believe that the tragedy in the church today is that the Holy Spirit *is* being restrained, grieved, quenched, or neglected.

So if I want to consider how the Holy Spirit can be restrained in my life I have to consider *how the Holy Spirit may be released* in my life. I need to make sure He's not to be a prisoner! I remember a very godly Scottish minister saying that the answer to the question, 'How do you grieve the Holy Spirit?' is this: We grieve the Holy Spirit when we fail to allow Him to do in us that for which He has been given. So when we're thinking of the operation of the Holy Spirit in our lives, there's a simple threefold distinction which I think we need to get hold of if we're not going to get confused.

First, there's *the life the Holy Spirit wants to live in me*. That's obvious — He's a Person. It is His own life! It's a Divine life! He is God, who is both love and light; and these characteristics of the divine Spirit will determine the life He wants to live. That means there'll be a whole lot of things He'll want out, and a whole lot of things He'll want to bring in; but there is a life He wants to live. I've got to let Him live that life.

Then of course there's *the gift He wants to give*. Our Bible makes that plain in 1 Corinthians 12; Ephesians 4; Romans 12; we've heard about that. But we need to remember both the diversity of the gifts and the sovereignty of the giver. Never, never, never, never, never tell anybody they ought to have any gift. It's quite wrong! And be very careful about claiming you have a gift. Some people claim the gift of being preachers, but the congregation disagree when they hear them preach!

No! You and I don't claim gifts — usually it is the church that sees them.

Then there's something else; there are *things He wants to do* in me. We call these the ministries of the Holy Spirit. And if you were to ask me what is the secret of the power of the Holy Spirit in a life, I would submit that it has little to do with the gifts. I can have the gift without the power. I can have the gift of preaching without the power of the Spirit quite easily, but if the Holy Spirit is not being allowed to do in me the things He's been given to do, then the power has gone! If I'm not allowing Him to live the life in me He wants to live, the power's gone, because I'm grieving Him. There is therefore one very important question that every Christian ought to ask — it is what does the Holy Spirit want to do in my life? What has He been given to do? Have you ever asked that question? Because there are things the Holy Spirit *has* been given to do.

I can only name them, we haven't got time to go into them in detail. But note that the difference between a gift and a ministry of the Spirit is that the gift is used occasionally and gifts differ from Christian to Christian. The ministries are in almost continual use, used far more frequently than the gifts, and are things that the Holy Spirit wants to do in *every* Christian.

He wants *to teach us*. Jesus spoke about that. John 14:26, 16:30. 'He will teach you.' Do you give Him the opportunity? The importance of spending time with your Bible is not to conform to a pattern of evangelical piety, it's in order that the Holy Spirit can teach you.

He's been given *to seal your life*. Paul says, 'When you believed, you were sealed with the Holy Spirit.' Dr Jowett says that a 'seal' primarily indicates ownership. One of the things the Holy Spirit wants to do in your life is to *bring everything under the authority of Jesus Christ*. That's one of the things He's been given to do.

The praying ministry, Romans 8:26. We don't know how or what to pray. He's been given to help us in private prayer and in corporate prayer. How much time do we give to that?

The caring ministry — we've lost sight of this! The love

of God,' says Paul, 'has been shed abroad in our hearts by the Holy Spirit given to us.' That love is not so much a gift of the Spirit — it is part of His very nature! He wants to care for others, and this, of course, is where a lot of our thinking about Christian love is sloppy and shallow. The biblical word 'agape' was very seldom used in classical Greek, and it always mean something *'infinitely precious'*, quite different from the word for physical love or human affection! It's in a different dimension altogether, it has within it a minimum of emotion, but a maximum of evaluation!

So the caring ministry means that people matter. But how many people really matter to you? A girl once said to me in one of my churches, 'The trouble with you people is that you're only interested in my soul. You want to see me converted.' Of course we did, but the trouble was that that was all we were interested in. We weren't interested in her as a person, but God was!

The leading ministry — 'as many as are led by the Spirit of Christ'. There's lots going on today that makes me think of Dr Paul Rees's phrase about Christians wanting to be 'big ducks in small puddles'. A leadership craze with much of self and little of the spirit!

And what about *testifying ministry*? 'He shall testify of Me.' I used to think that that meant that the Holy Spirit would testify to me about Christ, and I was right but I was also wrong. God not only wants to testify *to* me, He wants to testify *through* me. That means I've got to be ready to open my lips and my mouth! When did you last say a word for Jesus to anybody?

Well, there it is. The Holy Spirit can be restrained, *the Holy Spirit must be released*. We've thought of the variations in our lives and the purposes of God, the operation in our lives of the Spirit of God; finally and very briefly, let us consider:

The motivation in our lives of the fear of God

What kind of fear are we talking about? The fear of a tyrant, or the fear of a father of whose love we are so sure?

101

I love the story of the late Dr Barnhouse, that most dogmatic of all Presbyterian American preachers to preach at Keswick. He once asked a Roman Catholic priest, 'One thing bothers me about your church, that's the place you give to Mary the mother of our Lord. Why do you do it?'

The Roman Catholic priest thought for a moment and then said, 'If I were going to meet the King, I would like somebody to introduce me.'

'But not,' replied Dr Barnhouse, 'if the King was your father.' It is the fear of love. There is the thought here of *the failure that love will dread*. When I played cricket when I was young, I was always scared when I saw my father among the spectators. I wasn't afraid of the bowler. I was afraid of disappointing Dad! There is also here the thought of *the Father love would please*!

I think it was William Barclay who said that the highest motivation in life is 'to see the light in someone's eyes'. If you're a Mum or a Dad and you go to a school concert, you see your child in the choir looking this way and that; and then they see you, and they're content. They're not just there to sing as part of the choir. They're there to sing because you're there, and they want to give you delight.

I love that young people's hymn which begins

Just as I am, young, strong and free
To be the best that I can be,
For truth, and righteousness, and Thee
Lord of my life — I come.

The verse I love best is the last one,

And for thy sake to win renown,
And then to take the victor's crown,
And at thy feet to lay it down,
Lord of my life — I come.

I don't want to raise a great congregation to an emotional 'high'. I'm not interested in that kind of spiritual 'high'. There's a lot of it around today! I want us to get down to the nitty-gritty of how to be continually being filled with the Spirit. It's something I've got to watch very carefully every day of my life; and if I'm letting Him do what He's been given to do, I shall find that I am being filled. Maybe I won't notice it; but others will, and God will, and He'll start using me. Are you, am I, being filled? If that's what it means, these are the marks, this is the secret! Nothing very exciting, a bit down-to-earth, but that's what being a Christian, being filled with the Spirit, is all about.

Are we willing for the nitty-gritty business? Or do we just want the spiritual 'high'?

How reliable are you?
'*The fruit of the Spirit is . . . faithfulness*'. Galatians 5:22

In these days when there is so much talk about the person and work of the Holy Spirit, it is surely a matter for concern that so little stress is laid on the fruit of the Spirit, that which is the only sure evidence that the Holy Spirit is free to do His gracious work in the lives of God's people! I want to stress one facet of the fruit of the Spirit which is 'faithfulness.' In the AV it is translated 'faith,' indicating the problem we face in translating the Greek word here. It can mean either 'faith' or 'faithfulness,' as in the RSV. I would suggest that the' latter meaning is the true one.

When I came to dedicate my book, *Pastor and People, Studies in 2 Corinthians* — an epistle which deals almost entirely with the relationship between a pastor and his people — I wrote the following dedication; I dedicated the book with indescribable gratitude to 'The Faithful Church Member, that wonderful person whose praises go so largely unsung but without whose regular attendance, constant dependability, faithful intercession, lasting affection and unstinted generosity in the giving of time, money and strength, the work of the pastor would not be possible'.

A definition of faithfulness might not be out of place. We need to know the meaning of the words that we use so glibly. Here is a definition, 'firmness in adhering

103

to promises, to duty, to allegiances, etc . . . stability, reliability, fidelity. . .' The nature of these qualities may be made clearer when we state their opposites . . . 'instability, unreliability, infidelity.'

What then has the Word of God to say about 'faithfulness'? Why should it be one of the qualities of character and conduct that mark out the truly Spirit-filled and mature Christian?

How the divine Spirit creates faithfulness

I want us to note two lines of thought here. We are thinking in terms of a life in which *the ministries of the Holy Spirit are being exercised.* Whatever a person who is not a Christian may be, a person who is a Christian will have this unmistakable hallmark of faithfulness, of reliability! But for this quality to be produced the Holy Spirit must be at work in the life of such a Christian. A great deal of the confusion about the Spirit today is due to a failure to make three very simple but crucial distinctions between the life he will want to live in me, the gift or gifts He will want to give to me, and the things or ministries He will want to do and exercise in me! Concerning the last, Sister Eva of Friedenshort has written, 'in the lives of too many Christians the Holy Spirit is a prisoner without power.' He has been received, but He is not being allowed to do the things He has been given and wants to do in our lives! We are grieving the Spirit!

May I stress that this has nothing to do with the gifts of the Spirit. There is no question so urgent for any Christian as the question 'what has the Holy Spirit been given to do in my life, and am I allowing Him to do what He wants to do'? May I say again, this question deals not with possession of any gift of the Spirit, this has to do with His ministries. What those ministries are we can find out from the Word of God, if we want to!

The second line of thought means that we have to note that we are thinking of a life in which *the identity of the servant of God can be recognised.* If you want to know whether or not a Christian is truly and fully mature, look

104

for this quality. If it is absent, if the fruit is not to be seen, then you know that there is something basically and tragically wrong. Why can we affirm this? Simply because the Holy Spirit is the Spirit of God, and one of the basic qualities in the Godhead is *'faithfulness'*. How often we read of this in the Word of God: 'Thy faithfulness reacheth unto the clouds (Psalm 36:5). In Lamentations 3:23 we read 'great is Thy faithfulness' — words which have inspired one of our loveliest hymns 'Great is Thy faithfulness O God my Father, there is no shadow of turning with Thee'. If the God who indwells us by His Spirit is a faithful God, then we His children who possess that very nature must be seen to be faithful too! This is part of the 'family-likeness' that should be obvious and apparent where we work, in our homes or in the fellowship of other believers. Secondly let us note:

How the divine service demands faithfulness

Do we need to be reminded that the Christian has been 'saved to serve'. There is no hint in the Bible that what God does for us stops with us! Even in our thinking about the Holy Spirit, the same emphasis is found in Scripture. The promise of the power of the Spirit in Acts 1:8 was linked with the task of witnessing to the uttermost parts of the earth. In Christ's great utterance in the temple, the promise of the Spirit to those who thirsted and believed was that 'out of their inner being there would flow rivers of living water'. We seem to have got our understanding of the purpose of the Spirit all wrong today. In the minds of some it would seem that the Spirit has been given simply so that we can have a wonderful time, holding festivals, instead of doing a wonderful job!

Let us then be clear about *the involvement we should find in the service of our God*. Paul's favourite word to describe himself was as 'the servant of Jesus Christ'. Servants are there to serve. Peter writes of Christians as intended to be 'good stewards of the manifold grace of God'. When we pray 'Thy will be done' so often we think of this as something to be done to us *by* God, instead of something to be done *by us for God*. The will of God has personal implications, both positive and negative, but the will of God has universal implications. In 1 Timothy 2:4 Paul writes of 'God . . . who will have all men to be saved and to come to the knowledge of the truth. . .' and to make that possible. 'Christ Jesus . . . gave Himself a ransom for all'. And don't let any so-called theological reasoning contradict the plain statements of God's Word. Peter confirms this in 2 Peter 3:9 that 'The Lord . . . is not willing that any should perish but that all should come to repentance'. That is the service to which we are called and for which we are equipped with the power of the Spirit, that 'all men should be saved'!

Let us then also make sure that we are clear about *the requirement we must face in the service of our God*. 'It is required in stewards that a man be found *faithful*'. The steward is a man who has been entrusted *with* something *to do* something. We have been put in trust with the Gospel so that others may be saved. The basic qualification is that we should be faithful in discharging our responsibility in praying, in giving, in caring, in living and in speaking. Finally I want us to note:

How the divine Saviour rewards faithfulness

The parable recorded in Matthew 25:14–25 has the matter of faithfulness at its very heart, and when the servants came to have their work assessed by their Lord the assessment and the rewards had to do with whether or not they had been faithful. So there are two very simple considerations around which our thoughts can gather quite simply and shortly. The first is *what our service for God will reveal*, and that is whether or not we have been faithful. In the parable, the talents represent the opportunities given to us. The number of the opportunities varied with the abilities of the servants. Let's not forget that a judgment day is coming for the Christians, and that it will not be concerned with our sins (they were judged at Calvary) but it will deal with our service. God will assess then what we have done with all that God has entrusted to us. It will be, in my understanding, a day for surprises; something very different will emerge on that day. Some who thought they had done well will discover that they have not done as well as they and others had thought! And others who had felt that they had not done much will find out just how much God had been able to do with the service they had offered.

The second consideration is to note carefully *how the Saviour of men rewards*. The lovely thing about his is that I find that the Saviour rewards good and faithful work with more work! The smaller opportunities, the fewer opportunities faithfully grasped and used will bring more and greater opportunities. 'Thou hast been faithful over a few things, I will make thee ruler over many.' I used to think it a bit unfair when we read that the man who had done nothing had even that one talent, that one opportunity, withdrawn from him and given to another. But when you stop to think, that makes sense. Why waste opportunities by giving them to people who won't use them? No business man would do that, why should our Lord? Have you ever wondered why God seems to use some people much more than others. They may not be so gifted, but they are used of God. Here is the explanation, they have been found faithful. And faithfulness is something that God expects of us until we die. 'Be thou faithful unto death.'

7: Christian love . . . counterfeit or genuine?

Anything of real value is liable to be counterfeited, and therefore we should not be surprised if Christian love has its counterfeits. I remember vividly the embarrassment I felt when as a schoolboy I was on holiday in the Scottish Highlands at a place called Grantown-on-Spey. My Uncle Harry was on furlough from India where he had been a missionary for very many years. We had gone to the putting green and he had very kindly offered to pay for our round of putting. He handed in a pound note and received his change. It included a half-crown. Immediately he took it up and tapped in on the little counter and then handed it back to the girl at the desk. 'That's no good,' he said, 'please give me another one'. The girl was stunned with amazement, she had never had anyone speaking like that before. But my Uncle Harry had come back from India where there was a great amount of bad coinage in circulation, and there you never accepted silver without testing it to see if it was the real thing! I believe that it is more than time that the Christian Church started testing what is in circulation today in many areas under the guise of 'Christian' love, much of which is very open to question as to whether or not it is the real thing or a counterfeit. There is so much sloppy, sentimental, even sensual 'love' (can we even call it that?) in circulation today that needs to be examined to see if it is genuine 'Christian love'. The next two messages deal with some of the marks of the genuine article, which when possessed in the Spirit, will then penetrate and transform every other kind of love with its own distinct qualities.

The true nature of Christian love

'The fruit of the Spirit is love.' Galatians 5:22

The word love has been finding a prominent place in the vocabulary of the Christian Church today. Some time ago I watched a TV service from an Anglican Church of a higher churchmanship than my own. They had a break in the Communion Service in order to demonstrate their Christian 'love' for one another. They went around hugging and kissing one another. I found myself asking 'Was that what is meant by Christian love?' I found myself asking what would I have thought if I had seen that going on in a pub, or at a Rotary Lunch!! When the Pope visited Eire he stated that the solution to the problems between the north and the south could only be solved by 'love'. He did not however give any indication as to where that love was to come from! The New Testament speaks of love as being the distinctive mark of true Christian discipleship, 'By this shall all men know that ye are my disciples if ye have love one for another.' John 13:35. In 1 John 3:14 John states 'We know that we have passed from death unto life because we love. . .' While Paul writes in 1 Corinthians 13 that 'the greatest is love.' But what *is* Christian love?

It is important to realise that while in English we have only one word for love, in Greek there are three words, the word 'eros' from which we get our word erotic and which refers to sensual or sexual love; another word is 'phileo' which was the word commonly used to describe affection, a being fond of, the love between parents and children, between husband and wife, between friend and friend. But when the early Christians wanted a word to describe what Paul calls *'the love of God* which has been shed abroad in our hearts by the Holy Spirit given to us,' they chose another word, the word 'agape'. The IVF Bible Dictionary points out that this was a word very seldom used in classical Greek, except when it was used in connection with something *'infinitely precious'*. That being so then the definition of Christian love I heard from Dr Paul Rees is illuminating, 'the word,' he says, 'has within it *a minimum of emotion but a maximum of evaluation.*' Christian love is not so much a matter of hugging and kissing as a matter of recognising the value, the worth of a person, or a place or a thing! If the person is not important to me, then I don't hug them or kiss them! This definition I found of enormous help. It made 'loving' in the Christian way something more possible! I might find it hard to be fond of someone, but to recognise their value, their importance, their worth was different. What then is the true nature of Christian love? We will try to answer this in the light of the Scriptures by asking and trying to answer three questions.

When does this Christian love begin?

The answer in the Scriptures is full of encouragement. It speaks of Christian love as *something that has been given to me*. In Romans 5:5 Paul writes 'the love of God *has* been shed abroad in our hearts by the Holy Spirit which *has* been given to us.' We need to note exactly what Paul does say and not what some commentators say he said! Paul does *not* say 'our knowledge of the love of God', he says '*the love of God*'. He does *not* say 'our love for God', he says '*the love of God*'. The love which has been given to us, is *the very love of God*. It is a Divine love, the very love of God!! It only takes a moments thought to see how this is so. When I received the new life, the new love came with it. So I don't need to ask for this love, I have already received it. It is *not* a gift of the Spirit, love is part of the very nature of the Spirit. The two outstanding qualities of the Divine nature, so John tells us in his first epistle, are that 'God is love', and that 'God is light.' The emergence of this new love in our experience is part of the evidence that we have the new life, that we have been born again of the Holy Spirit. Recall again the words of St John in 1 John 3:14 'We know that we have passed from death unto life *because we love. . .*'

Keeping in mind that the sense of this 'agape' love is that it has within it a minimum of emotion but a maximum of evaluation our own experience bears

110

witness to the changes of values that come into our lives after we have become Christians. Before our conversion we did not value the Word of God, we never read it! After our conversion we realised its supreme value! Before our conversion we did not value the House of God, after our conversion we realised the supreme importance of the weekly time spent in worship and in fellowship there! Before our conversion we did not value, did not recognise the worth of Christians, we thought them peculiar and rather to be avoided. After our conversion we discovered their true value! I recall a student in one of our universities who had had little time for the church in her life. Some of her fellow students were concerned about her and were praying that she would become a Christian. One day she fell in love with another student and it seemed to be the real thing so she started looking round for a church that would be suitable for her wedding. Her friends had talked a lot about the church they went to and it seemed a possibility so she came out to my church in Edinburgh to see for herself. She started coming regularly and then at a service the crisis came and she found Christ for herself. Several weeks later I asked her how she was getting on, and got the reply 'Fine'. I then asked her how she was getting on with her Bible reading, and got the same reply. When I asked her what book in the Bible she was reading at that time she replied, 'the Book of Job'. 'What!' I said, and went on 'what about the New Testament?' 'Oh, I have read that right through!' The Bible which had meant little to her before, had now become something 'infinitely precious'!

But the Bible speaks of this 'agape' love not only as something that has been given to us, but as *something that should be growing in us*. cf Phil. 1:9 where Paul prays 'that your love may abound yet more and more.' 'In knowledge and in all judgment', 'in all discernment' (RSV) or 'in wise insight' (Phillips). This Divine love transforms our own human love and returns like a boomerang in a new quality of love for the Lord Himself. And the soil in which that love grows is the soil of knowledge. As we come to know Him more and more through His

Word, and through proving Him in the sufficiency of His grace, so we come to realise more and more His supreme worth! That is why in any church service where the Word of God is proclaimed in its fulness and truth, the highest point of worship comes at the end of the sermon, when as we have come to know Him better and have responded to His Word and will in fuller measure, and we therefore are giving Him more truly His worth in our lives, we are worshipping Him more truly than before. Singing may not have an ounce of worship in it however loud, repeated and prolonged it may be, if the words on our lips are not matched by a true response in our lives. Getting to know some-one depends on the amount of time we spend together and the number of things we do together. We can begin to understand why Paul in Phil. 3:10 puts knowing His Lord first in this statement of his threefold ambition, 'that I may know Him, and the power of His risen life, and the fellowship of His sufferings.' Paul had been captivated by a Person, wanted to be liberated by a power and was willing to be dominated by a purpose. The second question is this:

What does this Christian love become?

When I consult my Bible I find that this growing, deepening divine love has two results. First of all *it provides the motive of my service*: in 2 Cor. 5:14 Paul writes 'the love of Christ constraineth me.' Notice again exactly what Paul says, it is the 'love of Christ' that is constraining him. When we look at the highest qualities inherent in human love and add to them the distinctive qualities of Divine love we find our lives motivated in a degree that exceeds anything we have ever known before. One of the loveliest pictures in the New Testament of the best in human love is surely the incident recorded in St John's Gospel in the opening verses of the twelfth chapter when Mary anoints the feet of Jesus with that costly ointment the fragrance of which would be carried by Christ to the cross itself! Two words stand out as if written in gold, they are the words 'very costly', and speak to us of the sheer extravagance of love. Human love is extravagnt in the time it is willing to give, in the strength it is willing to spend, and in the price it is willing to pay. Human love is a great giver. Do you know the words of the poem which reads

Love ever gives,
Forgives, outlives
And ever stands
With open hands;
And while it lives it gives,
For this is love's prerogative
To give,
And give,
And give!

It is true too, of course, of the Divine love of which we read in John 3:16 that 'God so loved the world *that He gave. . . .*' He gave then and still gives! Most of us have seen the best and the highest in human love in the love that our mothers showered upon us. What ungrudging, unremitting service that was! What about our service for Jesus Christ — has that borne the same marks of extravagance?

This growing deepening divine love also *decides the measure of my surrender.* Years ago at the Keswick Convention in England I heard a memorable address given by the late Fred Mitchell which he titled 'Love's Consecration of all for ever.' It was based upon the words of the slave in the Old Testament days who after six years was faced with the choice of freedom or of continuing service. Some slaves might want to stay with a Master whom they had come to love and this was provided for in the words 'If the servant shall plainly say, 'I love my Master, I will not go out free', then the slave would serve the Master of his choice for ever! The motive for that surrender you will note was to be love. That sounds a hard thing to have to say. But is that not precisely what every bride and bridegroom say in their wedding service when asked the question 'Wilt thou take this man (this woman) to be thy wedded husband (wife) . . . and forsaking all others keep thee *only unto him (her) as long as ye both shall live?*' This is not the demand of a tyrant, but the desire of love which seeks all and gives all in return. One of the best known speakers and teachers of the Keswick Convention during the first forty years was the late Rev Evan Hopkins. He commented on the words of St Paul in Rom. 1:13 'Yield yourselves unto God as those that are alive from the dead.' He speaks of ceasing to resist the pleadings of love, ceasing to withhold ourselves from all that that love would want to do for us, and ceasing to struggle along without the help of that love. So the hymn writer speaks of the surrender of the Christian to the love of God in words most of us have sung many times

> In full and glad surrender
> I give myself to Thee,
> Thine utterly and always
> And evermore to be.

So when our Lord set out the terms of discipleship He said 'Whosoever he be of you that forsaketh not all that he hath, he cannot be my disciple.' Now I don't think that He meant that everything had to go *out of our lives*, but that everything had to go *out of our control* and into His!

We have asked and tried to answer two questions to help us to understand the meaning of true Christian love, when does this Christian love begin? and what does this Christian love become? The third question we have to ask and try to answer is:

How does this Christian love behave?

When I turn to my Bible I find two facets that are challenging and the first concerns *the perception that Christian love will display*. For this we turn again to the prayer of Paul for the Philippians and note that he prays that their 'love may abound yet more and more in knowledge and *in wise insight*.' That is the translation of J B Phillips, and I like it. One of the most common statements about human love is that love is blind. But while it may be true that love is blind to faults, and that is wide open to question as we shall see, love is not blind to *thoughts*. There is a perceptiveness about love, a sensitivity, a discernment. Love sees what others do not see. Turn back again to that story that we have already looked at in John 12, the story of the demonstration of the love of Mary for her Lord. That was supposed to be a festive occasion, a joyful time. But Mary knew that the thoughts in the mind of the Master she loved were only in part with those who were there. His thoughts were with the Cross under whose shadow He now walked and towards which He drew nearer with every step He took. Her love made her wise.

One of the memories I have of my childhood comes back to me. I never liked going to the dentist, in those days such visits were not too pleasant, mercifully things have changed a lot! If I had toothache I would not want to tell my mother as I knew that she would make an appointment for me to go to our dentist, so I said nothing. One evening I had raging toothache. I was sitting by the fire in our sitting-room, my mother was doing some mending and I was gazing into the fire. Then suddenly she spoke, 'Have you got toothache, George?' I had said nothing but she knew. One day a Christian lady had finished her shopping in the store and was checking out at one of the cash desks, the shop was quiet and there was no line of customers behind her. While the shop assistant was totting up the bill, this lady was watching the girl's face, and when she had paid her bill she said quietly to the girl, 'Is everything all right?' The girl looked up startled, and then burst into tears because everything was not all right! It took someone who cared to see and sense that she was in trouble. Yes, there is a perception that love will display.

But there is also *a Perfection that Love will demand*. We are wrong if we think that love will tolerate anything; love is more critical and more intolerant than we ever dream. Love demands perfection. Here is a girl getting ready for her wedding, what is her standard? Will anything do as far as her dress is concerned, as far as her appearance is concerned? Does getting ready for her wedding just take a few minutes of hurried preparation? Certainly not! Here is a young mother making garments for her firstborn child What is her standard? Is it not perfection? With what painstaking care the little garments are knitted. So it is in that prayer of St Paul for the church at Phillippi he prays that they might be 'sincere and without offence at the day of Christ.' If we want to know the perfection that love will demand of itself and of those it loves we have the standard set out in that matchless chapter in I Corinthian 13. Listen to what Paul has written there 'Love is very patient, very kind. Love knows no jealousy. Love makes no parade, gives itself no airs, is never rude, never selfish, never irritated, never resentful. Love is never glad when others go wrong but love is gladdened by goodness. Love is always slow to expose, always eager to believe the best, always hopeful, always patient. Love never disappears.' What a standard of perfection! What a shattering standard that is for so many who talk so glibly about Christian love today!

I always think of a story that I once heard about a small boy who was having a wonderful time making mud pies playing in the garden on a hot summers day. His dad came back from the office and went into the garden and collapsed into a chair. He was tired and he was hot. His little son looked at his dad and said 'Dad,' would you like a drink of iced water?' 'Would I not?' said his dad. The little fellow got up and went into the kitchen and took a jug of iced water out of the refrigerator and with his dirty muddy hands and fingers poured out a tumblerful and brought it to his dad, and to make sure that he did not spill it, he hooked one of his fingers over the lip of the glass and his finger went down into the water and the mud slipped off his finger and sank to the bottom of the tumbler! He gave it to his Dad who took it with the words, 'Thank you so much, son, that's just what I wanted, that's perfect!' The comment that followed that story, I have never forgotten, 'There was perfection there, a perfection not of achievement, but of intention', and that is what love is looking for.

'The fruit of the Spirit is love.' So Paul writes in

Galatians 5:22. Many commentators feel that there should be a semi-colon after that word 'love', and that what follows are facets of that love which alone is the final valid evidence that the Holy Spirit is filling our lives, and doing His gracious work in us. Someone who obviously felt that to be so wrote these words, and with them I close our study of the true meaning of Christian love.

> The Fruit of the Spirit is love:
> Joy is love exulting, and Peace is love at rest;
> Patience, love enduring in every trial and test;
> Gentleness, love yielding to all that is not sin;
> Goodness, love in action that flows from Christ within.
> Faithfulness, love's trustworthiness that all the world can see;
> Meekness, love not fighting, but bowed at Calvary;
> Temperance, love in harness and under Christ's control,
> For Christ is love in Person, and love, Christ in the soul.

How love can disturb
'*It is the voice of my beloved.*' Song of Solomon 5:2–6:10

Many years ago I came across a booklet that was entitled, if my memory is correct, 'Comfy Christians'. It was, I think, written by Miss Amy Wilson Carmichael of Dohnavur. She based it around the story of a little girl who had gone out to a party with the usual instructions from her mother to be a good girl. On her return her mother asked her, 'Have you been a good girl?' To which the girl replied, 'I haven't been good, I haven't been naughty, I've just been *comfy*!' This suggested to Amy Wilson Carmichael one of the dilemmas in the Christian church which is that too many Christians are just 'comfy Christians'. They are not particularly good Christians, not particularly bad Christians but simply 'comfy Christians'!

This passage in the Song of Solomon indicates how

disturbing, how uncomfortable the intrusion of the love of God can be. The Song of Solomon is admittedly one of the more difficult books of the Bible. Indeed there are some who think it ought not to be in the Bible at all! It is a story based upon the relationship of love between a royal bridegroom and his chosen but humble bride. Saints all down the centuries have however seen in this a parable of the relationship between Christ the Heavenly Bridegroom and His bride the Church. Although some parts of the book may be more difficult to understand than others, the passage before us is quite simple and clear in its messages. We can begin by noting:

The abundance that love bestows

We have here in these verses a picture of the bride at ease amid the lavish provision that love has made for her. She is at ease, at rest, relaxed, happy, and comfortable. In verse 5 she says, 'My hands dropped with myrrh and my fingers with sweet smelling myrrh.' Like the Psalmist the lines had fallen for her in pleasant places.

Here, right away, we find the Old Testament falling into line with the New Testament. We can see here illustrated *the enrichment Christ brings to life*. You will remember how Jesus said in John 10:10 'I am come that they might have life and that they might have it more abundantly.' I remember many years ago hearing the Rev. John R W Stott saying at Keswick, that 'no life is ever impoverished by being a Christian.' No life is ever the poorer because of Christ, and it is the devil's lie that proclaims otherwise. God's love is a giving love as all true love is. In John 3:16 we are told that 'God so loved the world that He gave.' He gave then, He still gives and gives and gives. There are, of course, forces that do impoverish our lives. Our Lord speaks of those in that same 10th chapter of John's gospel where He ways, 'The thief cometh not but for to steal and to kill and to destroy' but Christ is not a thief, and every single Christian who has accepted Christ would bear witness to the enrichment that He has brought into their lives. How rich life becomes when Christ comes in!

But not only is there here the thought of the enrichment that Christ brings to life, but of *the enjoyment Christ plans for life*. Some people have the strange thought that God's will is always unpleasant. But the Bible's witness is quite different. Paul writes to Timothy in 1 Tim. 6:17 of 'God who giveth us all things richly to enjoy.' In John 15:11 our Lord says, 'These things have I spoken unto you that my joy might remain in you and that your joy might be full.' The enrichment that Christ brings into our lives is designed for our enjoyment. Christ is no 'pale Galilean with a whole world gone grey at His breath.' There should be a glow, a radiance about the Christian.

But how tragically even some of us preachers misrepresent our Lord when we preach the gospel of God's grace with almost funereal solemnity. We call our message the gospel, and that means the 'good news'. How often we preach it as if it was the worst of news! This may in part be due to an emphasis found today in some theological thinking, a concept of the sovereignty of God which seems to exclude all thoughts of the Fatherhood of God and of the love of God. Yet it was of the Fatherhood of God that our Lord spoke so constantly!

I remember hearing a delightful story told about the late Dr Donald Gray Barnhouse of Philadelphia. He spoke frequently at the Keswick Convention. On one occasion when he was making his way to the big tent from the speaker's house, he passed, as he frequently did, the local Roman Catholic priest. Until that moment, they had simply passed one another with a polite 'Good morning' or 'Good afternoon'. On this occasion Dr Barnhouse stopped. He felt it wasn't right that two clergymen should simply greet each other that way and so, this time, he thought he would stop and speak. After they had exchanged greetings, Dr Barnhouse said, 'There is one thing that troubles me about your church and its teaching, that is the stress that you put upon Mary, the mother of our Lord. Why do you do that?' The Roman Catholic priest thought for a moment and then replied, 'Well, if I was wanting to meet the king, I would like to have somebody to introduce me to the king.' To which Dr Barnhouse replied, 'But not if the king was your father!' So just as earthly fathers plan in love for the enjoyment of their children, how much more shall our Heavenly Father.

And so we take into account not only the enrichment but also the enjoyment that we find in the abundance that the love of God bestows. And there is nothing wrong so far with the bride. She is simply at ease, in comfort, and content! All this because of what the bridegroom in his love has given to her! I want us to note secondly:

The disturbance that love creates

In v2 we read, 'It is the voice of my beloved that knocketh, saying, "Open to me, my love, for my head is filled with dew and my locks with the drops of the night." ' Christians believe in the love of God and then some attempt to make that love a kind of cushion upon which their thinking proceeds to go to sleep! We forget that there is nothing so disrupting, so disturbing, so demanding, so upsetting as love.

What contributes to this disturbance that love creates? In the first place we can note *the nature of the bridegroom*. We have looked upon the inside of that closed door, its warmth, its comfort, its ease! Now look at the one who stands without! He says this of himself, 'My head is filled with dew, my locks with the drops of the night.' He was a man of the fields and of the flocks, a man whose life was a life of toil, of toil that took him out in all weathers, at all hours! This shepherd king somehow did not fit in just then to the pattern of life inside. Inside, we have a picture of warmth, outside a picture of toil and work. How utterly incongruous this figure is, drenched with the rain and dew. How chilly, how challenging the summons he brings. But what is the nature of our Heavenly Bridegroom with His redeemer heart? Is He not too a man of toil at all hours? Yes! And in all weathers? His brow is not wet with dew, but with blood. His locks are not wet with the drops of the night but with the spittle of his foes who mocked Him.

But the nature of the bridegroom has to be related to *the need of the bridegroom*. 'Open to me' is his cry! His longing is for fellowship. He yearns for someone to commune with, to company with. He longs to come in to her, so that then she may go out with him to share his tasks and to share his thoughts. So, 'Open to me,' is his cry. How true all this is when we think in terms of our Heavenly Bridegroom. We read in the New Testament that 'He chose twelve that they should *be with Him*! Christ's need is for fellowship, indeed, God's need is for fellowship too. Is that not why He created man? Christ wants us to have fellowship with Him in His redemptive work in the world, and He wants us to share in all that that implies. How disturbing all this is, how demanding, how disrupting, how upsetting, how uncomfortable! 'Open to me,' is His cry.'

We have thought then of the abundance that love bestows, of the disturbance that love creates, and now let us note:

The reluctance that love confronts

One would have thought that there would have been an immediate response. But no, instead note *there is lethargy here*. The bride protests in v3, 'I have put off my coat, how should I put it on? I have washed my feet, how shall I defile them?' 'No, no,' she says, 'don't disturb me. I'm having a lovely time! Don't spoil everything by upsetting things, by asking me to open the door and then to go out with you into the night.' I wonder if this lethargy is sometimes reflected in our so-called Christian life today. Maybe it's Sunday night and we're sitting in comfort in a chair watching a play on the television. The rain is lashing against the windows. A glance at the clock shows it is time to go to church. But who wants to go out on a night like this? Oh, the lethargy, the laziness that marks the church today. The need for fellowship with Christ may sound out clearly, but is met with protest. Members are needed in the choir. Teachers are needed in the Sunday school. Donations are wanted for this work or that. And all that the call produces is protests! Service is too demanding! It is too upsetting!

Our cry is, 'Leave me alone, let me alone, let me enjoy my Christian experience.'

Yes there is lethargy here but more, *there is tragedy here*. For, at last she moves. In v5 we read, 'I rose up to open for my beloved, and my hands dropped with myrrh, my fingers with sweet smelling myrrh upon the handles of the lock. I opened to my beloved, but my beloved had withdrawn himself and was gone. I sought him, but I could not find him.' She did respond, but it was too late! The shepherd king was gone! The relationship was still there but the fellowship was broken. It is, of course, possible to be a Christian and yet to be out of touch with our Lord. 'I sought him, but I could not find him.'

We have thought of the abundance that love bestows, of the disturbance that love creates, of the reluctance that love confronts and then let us note:

The experience that love permits

The Bible says that 'the way of the transgressor is hard.' It is mercifully so. God sees that it is never easy to disobey His will. Life then became very very difficult for the bride. We can see this, first of all in *the way she was treated*. In v7 as she seeks for the bridegroom we read, 'The watchmen that went about the city found me, they smote me, they wounded me, the keepers of the walls took away my veil from me.' The world has no time, no respect, for the Christian who is out of fellowship with his Lord, and, so, the bride finds the going rough. The treatment at the hands of the world was not kindly. And this was not because she was a good bride, but because she had failed in her relationship. Sometimes when Christians find the going rough, they are tempted to say, 'This is part of the price of being a Christian.' But sometimes that may not be true. It is not the price of being a Christian, it is the price of being a poor Christian. The world knows only too well the kind of life the Christian ought to live, the world knows perfectly well when things have gone wrong.

Not only do we see the experience that love permits

in the way she was treated but also in *the way she was troubled*. In v6 we read 'my soul failed'. In v8 we read, 'I am sick with love.' The whole thing was making her ill. Do you remember the words of that lovely hymn that begins 'Oh for a closer walk with God, a calm and peaceful frame'? You may remember one verse goes like this:

Where is the blessedness I knew,
When first I saw the Lord,
Where is the soul refreshing view
Of Jesus and His word?

What peaceful hours I once enjoyed,
How sweet their memory still,
But they have left an aching void,
The world can never fill.

Yes the bride was desperately unhappy because the bridegroom had gone. I believe there is what we might call a discipline of withdrawal in God's dealings with His people. Do you remember how in Hosea 4:17 we read of God speaking of Ephraim as being 'joined to idols' and then He says 'let him alone'. That can be understood either to mean that God was telling Judah to leave Ephraim alone, or that God was saying that He was going to leave Ephraim alone! But in either case, Ephraim was going to be left alone. Sometimes there may be the difficult experience in our lives of God withdrawing, not His presence, but the sense of His presence, so that we might realise that we just cannot live without Him.

So finally we come to the end of this very wonderful parable of the relationship between the heavenly bridegroom and his humble bride and the story ends on a happy note because we find in the end what I have called

The repentance that love rewards

There are two things that blend together here. The first is *the conviction the bride had reached*. And the conviction was that she could not live without the bridegroom. To lose him, was in a sense, to find him! Because it was only when she discovered what life was like without him that she knew she must have him. So when she was challenged by the daughters of Jerusalem in v9, in the words, 'What is thy beloved more than another beloved?' the bride replies that he is to her, 'the chiefest among ten thousand, the altogether lovely one.' There was such deep conviction in her soul about his worth to her that it brought such a testimony to her lips, that it aroused a longing in those to whom she speaks and they replied in chapter 6:1 'Whither is thy beloved gone that we may seek him with thee?'

The conviction she had reached leads on to the thought of *the companion the bride must have*. So she asks the question, 'Whither is he gone?' and receives the answer, 'to his garden to pasture his flock among the lilies.' In other words she would find him where she would always find him, at work. He would not come to her but if she would find him, and she knew she would, it would be if she went to him and joined him in the place of toil where his heart was set, where he would be busy meeting the needs of the flock! And, oh, the welcome she got! The bridegroom speaks now so tenderly to her of her beauty, 'Thou art beautiful' in chapter 6:4. The fellowship that had gone was restored, and hand in hand, they worked together!

I wonder if you have ever come across the words of a poem with which I want to end this message. This is how the poem reads:

I said, 'Let me walk in the fields.'
God said, 'No, walk in the town.'
I said, 'There are no flowers there.'
He said, 'No flowers, but a crown.'
I said, 'But the sky is black, there is nothing but noise and din.'
He wept as He sent me back
'There is more,' He said,
'There is sin.'
I said, 'But the air is thick, and fog is veiling the sun.'

He answered, 'Yet souls are sick, and souls in the dark
undone.'
I said, 'I shall miss the light, and friends shall miss
me, they say.'
He answered, 'Choose, you, tonight, if I am to miss
you, or they.'
I pleaded for time to be given.
He said, 'Is it hard to decide?
It will not seem hard in Heaven,
To have followed the steps of your guide.'
I cast one look at the fields,
Then set my face to the town.
He said, 'My child, do you yield.
Will you leave the flowers for the crown?'
Then into His Hands went mine.
And into my heart came He.
And I walk in the light divine —
The path I had feared to see.

8: How relevant is my faith in meeting the needs of people today?

Right at the very heart of the Christian Gospel lies the claim that it provides the answer to the most basic and vital question to which man has to find an answer, and that question is 'How can man get right with God?'. The answer, so the Christian claims lies in what Christ has done for man in His death on the Cross. There we are to 'behold the Lamb of God that taketh away the sins of the World.' But while the Cross lies at the very heart of the gospel, there are other needs in the hearts of men to which Christ and Christ alone will provide the answer. Canon Michael Green in one of his books quotes two statements which are worth noting; one is a statement made by a student. 'I want a God I can understand, who answers some of my deepest questions.' The other statement by another student runs, 'No God is worth preserving unless He is of some use in curing the illnesses which plague humanity!' I would agree. Someone has put it like this, 'While there is only one way to God, and that is through Christ, there are a thousand ways to Christ'. And whatever road we take that brings us initially to Christ, We find Him to be the One who not only died for our sins, but who as a risen Lord wants to enter our lives and bring into our lives all that the grace of God has to offer to meet our every need. If I was in business and had the job of being a trade representative, I would want to be convinced of the quality and relevance of the goods I was trying to get sold on the markets of the world. The two following messages indi-

cate two areas in which Christ can and will meet some
of these other needs.

How God can bring back loveliness into living

'*He will beautify the meek with salvation.*' Psalm 149:4

Contrary to the popular misconception of the nature
of the true Christian experience which thinks of it as
something drab and grey, out of which all the colour and
sparkle has been drained away, the Christian experience
brings into life qualities of colour and beauty that can
be obtained in no other way! The lines of the poet Swin-
burn are blasphemous when he speaks of Christ as that
'pale Galilean' and adds 'the world has grown grey from
Thy breath.' What arrant nonsense! In a day when the
world and the individual lives of men, women and children are increasingly being robbed of all beauty, the
Christian Gospel steps in with a ringing challenge that
God 'will beautify the meek with salvation.' The tragedy
is that so many Christians have failed to realise this,
their lives are not demonstrating or fulfilling the divine
intention.

Let us listen to the witness of the Scriptures. We have
noted already the words of the Psalmist, but elsewhere
in the Psalms this characteristic is stressed. In Psalm
9:17 we have the prayer 'Let *the beauty* of the Lord our
God be upon us.' In Psalm 29:2 we are commanded to
'Worship the Lord in *the beauty* of holiness.' The prophet
Isaiah speaking of the mission of the coming Messiah in
Isa. 61:3 says that He would give '*beauty* for ashes.' In
Jeremiah 18:1–6 the relationship between God and His
people is set out as being like that of the potter to the
clay. When we read of the potter that 'behold he wrought
a work in the clay,' and ask what the intention in the
mind of the potter might be, we find that the potter has
only two intentions in his moulding of the clay. He
intends either to make something that will be useful, or
to make something that is beautiful! In the New Testament Peter, in 1 Peter 3:3 speaks of the beauty of women

as being something to do not so much with 'outward adornment, but that of your inner self, the unfading *beauty* of a gentle and quiet spirit.' Here in our text we see and hear of the same truth that God 'will beautify the meek with salvation.' And I see nothing wrong with the translation as it stands in the Authorised Version! Let us consider then first of all what I have called:

The Divine intention

God's people are meant to be lovely people to look at and lovely people to live with, and their homes are meant to be the same. Let us note that *There is a love of beauty that we share with God.* The Bible tells us that God 'made man in His own image.' And we believe that although man has fallen by his sin, yet traces of that Divine image remain, and I believe that among these is an instinctive love of beauty. When God created the world He stamped it with beauty. Bishop Taylor Smith described nature as 'God's revelation of Himself in form and colour!' As the hymn writer puts it, 'every prospect pleases and only man is vile.'

We find beauty everywhere, in every land, in God's natural creation. And it seems logical to conclude that if beauty is found in creation, it will also be found in the character of the Creator! In my world travels I have found beauty everywhere. I have seen the sun setting in a sea turned to crimson, in a sky ablaze with glory at Hout Bay in South Africa! I have walked along the sun-drenched beaches of Honolulu. I have seen the beauty of snow-capped Mount Fuji mirrored in the still waters of Lake Ashi in Japan. I have gazed at the beauty of the Blue Mountains in Australia, the towering majestics peaks of the Alps in Austria and Switzerland soaring into the blue skies, or the Rockies in Western Canada and the Western States of America. And what shall I say of the beauty of my own Scottish Highlands, that blending of heather and bracken, silver birch and pine, mountain and moor, river and loch that make Scotland, for me, the loveliest country in the world. And what shall I say too of the softer beauty of the English Lake District, the beauty of the primrose and violet growing on the banks of an English lane, or the mist of bluebells carpeting the floor of some woodland in Spring? What shall we say of the beauty to be seen in the face of a bride on her wedding day, or the unspoilt beauty to be seen in the face of a child? Yes, we find beauty everywhere.

We want beauty for ourselves. We want it in our homes, so we buy new curtains, or re-decorate this room or that. We want beauty in our gardens so we work hard to see that in the summer there will be a beauty of colour or fragrance everywhere for us and for our friends to enjoy. We want it for our children, so we take infinite pains to see that they are healthy. We dress them as expensively as we can afford, indeed so often going beyond what we can afford. We want it for ourselves, and the ladies in particular will go to great trouble to be as attractive in dress and appearance as is possible, and their husbands are happy to have it that way. All this is natural and can be right. There is indeed a love of beauty that we share with God, and the Divine intention in the Creator who has created so much beauty in His natural creation, would not have it any other way!

But tell me this, is there not *a loss of beauty that we see in life?* As the hymn writer has put it, 'every prospect pleases *but only man is vile.*' Yes beauty can be lost, it can be destroyed. It can vanish from the countryside. In our land there are conservation groups keeping a watchful eye lest a beauty spot be lost through the inroads of industry. Beauty can die out of a marriage and home. Two young people who on their wedding day each thought the other absolutely fabulous, can some- times alas, all too soon reach the stage when they cannot stand the sight of one another! Beauty can sometimes die out of the face of a child! In our so called modern world beauty can die out of art, out of music! Is this a reflection of the fact that beauty can die out of the soul? We fight against this loss of beauty, we may weep over it!

But what is it that defaces, that defiles? The Bible will answer in just one word and that word is sin. When Christ diagnosed that the source of sin came from within,

129

He spoke of the way in which sin 'defiles!' Name any sin you like and there is nothing beautiful about it. There is nothing beautiful about temper or hatred, there is nothing beautiful about jealousy or greed, about selfishness or pride, about lying or drunkenness, about gossip or adultery! Dr Fosdick, a famous American preacher in his day, belonging to a more liberal school of theology than I myself, has written some devastating words about this aspect of sin. He writes, 'Sinful pleasure lures us only in anticipation, dancing before us like Salome before her uncle Herod, quite irresistible in fascination. Happiness seems altogether to depend upon an evil deed. But on the day that deed long held in alluring expectation is actually done, how swift and terrible the alteration in its aspect! *It passes from anticipation through committal into memory and will never be beautiful again!*' Or as the old puritan preacher, Gurnall, puts it in his book *The Christian Armour*, 'Faith sees sin before its finery be on and it be dressed for the stage, to be but a brat from hell, bringing hell with it.'

Here I believe is just one aspect, and a vital one at that, of the relevance of the gospel to meet one of the tragic and basic needs of men and women today. If Jesus Christ can deal with what takes beauty out of life, if Christ can bring loveliness back into living, into lives, and into homes, then surely here there is indeed 'good news'. So we must then consider what we find in our text concerning this. We have realised that the Divine Intention for life is that it should be beautiful, our text goes on to speak of:

The Divine provision

'He will beautify the meek *with salvation*.' Here is the Divine remedy, beauty can be restored by 'salvation'. But what is salvation? That is not a word that is often heard on the lips of people in their everyday speech. The BBC some years ago put on a series of TV programmes during Holy Week. The series was entitled 'Simple Faith'. The producer David Winter stopped ordinary people in the streets and asked them if they understood what some of the words meant that are familiar to most Christians. The Archbishop of Canterbury, at that time Dr Coggan, then closed the programme by giving an explanation of what the words did mean! One night the word was 'salvation'. Not a single person interviewed by David Winter had the faintest idea what the Christian understood by the word 'salvation'. So utterly pagan has England become! But while we may not be familiar with the word 'salvation', we do use the word 'save'. I could say quite honestly that there was a time when the drug penicillin 'saved' my life. We talk about someone being 'saved' from drowning. Supposing we used the word in our text as indicating 'God's saving help', that might bring the word and its meaning more understandably before us. When we turn to the Scriptures we find two simple facts about the Christian meaning of the word.

Salvation in the Scriptures is presented to us as (a) *something wrapped up in a Person*. Every Christmas we are reminded of this when we recall the message to Joseph concerning Mary's child. 'Thou shalt call His name Jesus for *He* shall *save* His people from their sins.' Salvation is not something to be found in the Church, it is not something to do with the Creeds, it is not something that depends upon conduct. Each and all of these will be implicated indirectly with God's saving work. But salvation has something to do *with Christ*! He Himself said '*I* am come to seek and to *save* that which is lost.' Some of us were brought up to sing some choruses the words of which have been implanted indelibly in our memories. One went like this:

> He did not come to judge the world,
> He did not come to blame;
> He did not only come to seek,
> It was to save He came;
> And when we call Him, Saviour,
> And when we call Him Saviour.
> And when we call Him Saviour
> Then we call Him by His Name!

That saving work had to do with Him dying for our sins

131

upon the Cross, but with more than that, it has to do with His coming to dwell in our hearts by His Spirit, when we ask Him to come in in His risen life and power! John tells us that 'To as many as received Him to them gave He the right to become the children of God.' Salvation then has to do with Christ dying for me to deal with the guilt of my sin, and with Christ dwelling in my life by His Spirit, to deal with its power.

But Salvation in the Scriptures is not only presented to us as something wrapped up in a person, but also (b) as *Something worked out in a Process*. When Paul wrote to the church at Corinth he spoke of this in 2 Cor. 3:18, 'all we beholding as in a glass the glory of the Lord, are being changed into His likeness from one degree of glory to another.' What a difference it makes when another life comes into our life. When a confirmed bachelor finally yields to the charm of a lady and she enters his life as his wife, then changes come fast and furious! There may be some things that will have to go out of his life, and there will no doubt be many more that will come in! What changes come when a child comes into the home, again the same procedure takes place, some things have to go out, and many more will come in! If that be so in our human experiences how much more will it be so when the very Son of God comes to dwell in a human heart and life by His Spirit! The one basic difference will be that every change will be dictated by perfect wisdom, perfect love, and perfect power. There will be a wisdom now that makes no mistakes, a love that never lets go or gives up, and a power that will never accept any defeat! No wonder Paul wrote that if any man be in Christ he is a new creature.' So the process of 'being saved' will go on and on 'till we all come in the unity of faith and of the knowledge of the Son of God, unto a perfect (mature) man, unto the measure of the stature of the fullness of Christ.'

We have thought of the Divine Intention and of the Divine Provision. We have yet to consider one other word in our text, the full text reads 'He will beautify *the meek* with salvation.' Here we face what I have called:

The divine condition

The first and the worst of sins is pride, and that is ultimately the sin that will keep a man back from experiencing all that the love and grace of God can do in us, for us and through us. To know anything at all of this transforming grace in our lives we have to be (*a*) *Humble enough to admit our need of Him*. The Scripture makes it plain that God 'giveth grace to the humble' and at the same time that He 'resisteth the proud.' How slow man is to admit his need before God as a sinner! It is one thing to know it, it is another thing to admit and to come humbly before God admitting our guilt, and our weakness! The Bible maintains that man is born in sin, not that there was anything sinful about his birth, but that there was something sinful about him at his birth! We really don't need the Bible to tell us that 'we have all sinned and come short of the glory of God.' Many years ago when Dr Temple was Archbishop of York, he chose as his book for Lenten reading one by Dr D R Davies. It was titled, 'The Secular Illusion or Christian Realism.' The Secular Illusion being that man is born naturally good, Christian Realism stating that man is not born naturally good, but is born a sinner. As a little girl in my Sunday School at Cockfosters put it to her mother, 'Mummy, why is it that there is something inside me that likes being naughty?' The Bible answers that while man was created good, man fell by his sin, and ever since then the heredity of sin has affected human nature. While studying Moral Philosophy at Edinburgh under Prof. A E Taylor who was reckoned at that time to have one of the most acute minds in Europe, and whose spiritual pilgrimage had been from agnosticism as a student to orthodox Christianity as a mature thinker, my attention was suddenly arrested when the Professor paused in his lecture and then said 'Ladies and Gentlemen please remember this, there must have been an Adam!' By that we presumed that what he meant was that there must have been a time when man first sinned!

Man is sinful and guilty too and he needs to be humble enough to admit his need not only initially, but continually. Man is not wise enough, not strong enough, not good enough, not loving enough, man as he is just cannot cope. He needs to be saved! How humbling, but how true!

But man also needs to be (b) *Humble enough to submit his will to Christ.* How pathetic are the results of those who pin their faith upon human remedies like education! Man's problem is not simply that he does not know what is right, but even when he does know what is right, he does not necessarily want to do it. You only need an alarm clock on a cold morning to tell you that. When my alarm goes off it tells me what is the right course of action to take, and that is to get up out of my bed. My problem however is that although I know that, I don't want to do it! And if I do, poor creature that I am, I don't have the power to get up out of my bed! So as a Christian I need to learn not only a whole new way of life, but I need to allow the now indwelling Lord to enable me to do what I otherwise could not do. When Paul tried to assess the new resources that the Christian has in Christ, he ran out of words that would describe the new resources, he writes of 'the riches of His grace', 'the exceeding riches of His grace' and then 'the unsearchable riches of His grace.' When a person becomes a Christian it is like a pauper marrying a millionaire! But the One Who died on the Cross for the forgiveness of my sins, and Who now dwells in me by His spirit in His risen power, is not only Saviour, He is Lord. And if I am to experience all that He is willing and able to do for me, in me and through me, then I must find out how He wants me to live, what He wants me to do or not to do, what He has provided for me in the means on grace, the Scriptures of truth, the ministry of the Spirit, the fellowship of the redeemed, and live a life of obedience to His perfect will. The Christian life is after all, the life of Christ being lived out in me by Christ Himself. The Christian is someone who can say 'I live, yet not I myself alone any more, but Christ liveth in me.'

One of the loveliest of all hymns begins like this:

May the mind of Christ my Saviour live in me from
day to day
By His love and power controlling all I do and say.

The last verse says:

May His beauty rest upon me as I seek the lost to
win,
And may they forget the channel, seeing only Him.

And when that happens then the words of our text will
indeed come true and 'He will indeed beautify the meek
with salvation'.

Man's search for happiness
Luke 15:11–24

This parable, known familiarly as the parable of the
prodigal son, is possibly the best known of all the
parables of Jesus Christ. It has been called 'the greatest
short story in the world'. But the title 'the prodigal son'
is possibly a title that may not make it seem relevant to
us. I prefer to call it 'man's search for happiness'. For
that is really what it's all about.

Two memories come back to me over the years. One
is the title of a thesis that we had to write in the class of
Moral Philosophy in Edinburgh University. The title
was 'Is happiness the only thing we desire?' I can't
remember what I wrote but I am quite certain that happiness is at least one of the more important things we
desire! The other memory is that of a sermon preached
by Professor James S. Stewart, at that time minister of
Beechgrove Church, Aberdeen. His text was 'Happy art
thou, oh Israel, who is like unto thee, oh people, saved
by the Lord' (Deut. 33:29). He titled his sermon 'Why
be a Christian?' The first reason he gave was because
'the Christian life is a happier life than any other', and

135

so it is! So I want to examine this story which reveals in a masterly way the insight of Jesus Christ into the needs of the human heart. Will you note with me first of all:

The desires that mastered the younger son

The desire of the younger son was very simply to get away from the presence and the authority of his father so that he might live his life in his own way. He didn't mind his father being alive as long as he did not exercise any authority over his own life! Is that not the attitude of many towards God? They are prepared to believe in the existence of God and may even acknowledge that belief by coming to His house on Sunday but they don't want God to interfere with their lives at any point whatever.

There are three things we can note in the desires of this younger son, first of all that *he was selfish*. The attitude of the younger son is summed up in two words 'give me'. That was what he said to his father and, turning to the glittering world that beckoned him, 'give me' was his attitude to that! In his life there was one way traffic, everything was going to come in. That attitude is still common today. So many people are living their lives on the principle of getting — getting money, getting excitement, getting popularity, getting their own way, getting everything they want for themselves. That is basically of course pure selfishness, but, tell me, is that not tragically common today?

The second thing to note about his desires was that *he was sincere*. I am sure he was sincere in his belief that happiness and freedom were to be found away from the father's presence and control, just as hundreds of people today are equally sincere in their belief that happiness and freedom are to be found by turning their backs upon God. But of course we don't want to make the mistake of thinking that sincerity and truth are the same thing. Many of us have memories of examinations when in all sincerity we wrote our answers to the questions but our sincerity did not mean that our answers were true and correct as maybe we found out to our cost! There's a

136

verse in Proverbs (16:25) which tells us 'There is a way that seemeth right to a man but the end thereof are the ways of death.' So, he was selfish, and he was sincere!

I am quite certain also that *he was stubborn*. Somehow I don't think that the father let him go easily. I am sure that again and again he pleaded and reasoned with his son, just as God never lets us go easily! Again the book of Proverbs tells us that 'the way of the transgressor is hard!' It is made hard of deliberate purpose because God knows that that way will never lead to happiness. In a score of ways the Spirit of God will plead with us. All of us here have known something of that. We have experienced the pricking of conscience, we've been stirred and rebuked by memories of the past. We've been challenged by the example of friends. Even the sight of a church or indeed of a clergyman can be used by God to halt us in our headlong rush away from Him. How extremely modern and how exactly accurate the diagnosis by Jesus Christ is in this parable of long ago. The younger son was selfish, he was sincere and he was stubborn! The desires that mastered him are the desires that master so many of us today!

I want us then to note what I have called:

The disasters that met him

It is here that the masterly touch of Jesus Christ is revealed. The correspondence between the parable and life is exact. This young man set out to get and immediately he began to lose. The first thing we note is that he *lost his wealth*. We read 'he wasted his substance' and 'he spent all'. Nothing is more certain than the fact that men or women, young or old, who turn their backs upon God, while contented maybe to acknowledge His existence, will lose their wealth. They will lose the really precious and valuable things that life can hold. I don't, of course, mean that they lose their money, for true wealth does not consist in nor can be bought with money. What is the wealth, what is the precious thing that life offers? Surely the most precious thing that life offers lies in the opportunities that life holds of being someone worth being, of doing something worth doing, of living a life worth living for the eternal good of others and the eternal glory of God? Think for a moment of the opportunity that so many have in their youth of building a truly lovely Christian home where the life and power of Jesus Christ give life that distinctive quality that nothing can counterfeit. The home where the hearts and lives of little children open up to the love of God in Christ like flowers to the sun. To lose the opportunity of knowing something of that is to lose wealth indeed.

So we note that he lost his wealth but also we note *he lost his freedom*. The very thing he set out to find, to demonstrate, to enjoy was the very thing he lost. So we read 'he went and joined himself to a citizen of that country and he sent him into his fields to feed swine.' The son of the father has become the slave of the foreigner. Freedom has been changed into fetters. And so it is with the men or women who today turn their backs upon God and not only lose their wealth but their freedom too. There is much stupid and shallow talk about freedom today. People talk about wanting to be free to do as they like. I think it was Dr Fosdick, the great American preacher, who said 'we may want to be free to do as we like but soon discover we are not free to stop doing it!' Peter in his second epistle writes of those 'who promise freedom and all the time they themselves are slaves!' How many there are who have lost their freedom.

It may be they are *in bondage to opinion they dare not flout*. The Old Book tells us that 'the fear of man bringeth a snare' (Proverbs 29:25) and scores of people are snared by the fear of man, shackled to the opinions and approval of the social circle in which they move. They dare not do the thing they know is right which, deep down, they want to do, because they are afraid, afraid of the raised eyebrow, the suppressed laugh, the whispered comment. Free? Their freedom is that of a goat, tethered to a post by a long rope. So often I have seen goats in the Highlands of Scotland tied like that, free only within the limits of the rope by which they are bound.

Others have lost their freedom because they are *in*

bondage to habits they cannot break. It was David the King who cried out once, in Psalm 65:3 'my sins are mightier than I' and Christ himself warned us in John 8:34 'whosoever committeth sin is the slave of sin.' Thousands today demonstrate the simple fact that, while men may like to think they are free to do as they like, they are not free to stop doing it. The power of sin to become habitual is a simple fact of experience.

But yet others have lost their freedom because they are *in bondage to consequences they cannot undo.* Life isn't a game and one of the most terrifying laws in the moral and spiritual realm is that which says, in Galatians 6:7 'Be not deceived, God is not mocked. For whatsoever a man soweth that shall he also reap.' As Professor Henry Drummond used to say to the students of Edinburgh 'Not only do we sow, we watch it grow. We see it ripen and then at last we reap.' And the tragedy is that so often others have to share in the reaping. When we were young my father used to take us as a family for our summer holiday to Speyside in the Scottish Highlands. We used to cycle a lot until we knew every road and every path through the forests and through the heather. Sometimes we would come to a small loch lying beside the road. There on a still, hot summer's day we would see reflected in the still surface of the water all the blended beauty of the heather, the silver birch, the pine tree and the bracken, the blue of the sky behind the massive rounded shoulders of some of the great mountains in Scotland. Boylike, I would search for a stone and throw it out into the centre of the loch where it would fall with a splash. In a moment the picture was shattered and from the centre an ever-widening circle of the ripples spread until the surface in every corner of the loch was quivering. I suppose it might have been possible to get the stone out again but nothing could stop the ripples spreading! Life is like that, nothing can stop the ripples spreading. What mockery then to talk of freedom.

He lost his wealth, he lost his freedom and *he lost his self-respect.* By that I mean his belief in his own worth to his own father. Listen as he speaks 'I shall say to him,

'Father I have sinned and *am no more worthy to be called thy son*." ' That is the final disaster that awaits the soul that follows the same road. When we come to think that, while others could be Christians, we never could, we have gone too far, we have left it too late, we have been away too long. Thank God it isn't true! It is part at least of the work of the Cross to give the lie to that, for one of the glories of the Cross is this, that 'God commendeth his love to us in that while we were yet sinners Christ died for us.'

We have thought then of the desires that mastered him, of the disaster that met him and then, finally:

The discoveries that made him

There were three, first of all *he discovered the failure he was*! In v17 we read 'he came to himself', he discovered himself and what a discovery that was! There he was, a Jew, feeding pigs and eating their food and, of course, to a Jew a pig was an unclean animal and a Jew could sink to no lower depths of shame than to be a swineherd. All his dreams had come to this, he had thought himself wise, he had been proved a fool, he had thought himself strong, he had been proved to be weak, he had sought happiness and had found misery, he had started out rich and had ended a pauper. Sometimes it is still the same with men today, it is not until we have surrounded our lives with things and people and standards that, in our truest moments we utterly despise, that we wake up and discover our true selves. He discovered the failure he was!

The second discovery he made was not only his folly but *he discovered the father he had*! In v20 we read 'He came to his father.' It is not enough to discover our need, we must seek the remedy and the soul that turns back to seek God makes the same discovery that the younger son made in this story told so long ago. What kind of a father did he have? Was he a kind of tyrant, a kind of spoil sport? Not a bit of it. He found his father was a giving and a loving father. So many people seem to think that becoming a Christian means giving up everything. I suppose in a sense we do give up some things, things that are not worth having, but becoming a Christian is not a matter of giving up, it is a matter of giving in, giving in to the love of God. And so we read 'When he was yet a great way off his father saw him and had compassion and ran and fell on his neck and kissed him.' When we throw the kiss of forgiveness in the parable on to the screen of history, *the kiss becomes a cross* and forgiveness is of course the first and the greatest of all the gifts that God gives to us! Our God is a giving God, for that is what love is, love is always a giver. Years ago I heard a saintly, godly Baptist minister saying 'Jesus is not a thief:' I remember hearing Dr John Stott of All Souls, Langham Place in London, saying 'No life is ever the poorer for becoming a Christian.' But of course the kiss of forgiveness was only the beginning of the giving, of the love of his father. We read after that the father said, 'Bring forth the best robe and put it on him and put the ring on his hand and shoes on his feet. Bring hither the fatted calf and kill it and let us eat and be merry.' God has so much to give us, everything that there is in Christ that we need is ours for the taking for 'the gift of God is eternal life.' Have you discovered the Father you have in God? He discovered the failure he was, he discovered the father he had!

He also discovered the fulness he sought! His real place, the future was not among the pigs, it was at the father's table in the father's presence doing the father's will. He was not meant to be a slave but a son. Is it not one of our poets who speaks of those who should be kings but are slaves? Well, kings maybe, but basically sons of God. I remember hearing of an old Scots minister who had his own threefold divisions as he told the story of the prodigal son. Using the softer Scottish word for home which is 'hame', he spoke of the younger son as being sick of hame, then of being hamesick, and then of being hame!

We have thought then of and found here in this parable a picture of a man's search for happiness that ended in failure until he came back to God the Father. We have thought of the desires that mastered him, he was selfish, he was sincere, he was stubborn. We have thought of the disasters that met him, he lost his freedom, he lost his wealth, he lost his self-respect and we have thought of the discovery that made him, when he discovered the failure he was when he discovered the father he had and when he discovered the fulness he sought! And that was as a son of the father, living in the father's presence, resting in the father's love and doing the father's will. No wonder one of the fathers of the Church wrote long ago, 'Thou hast made us for thyself and our hearts are restless until they find their rest in thee.'

9: How effective is our witness?

'Ye shall be witnesses unto Me' was the final word of the risen Christ to His Church. A witness has something to say and something to show. And the power of the Spirit was promised to use that witness to bring new life not only to ourselves but also to others. On my first and recent visit to South Korea I was amazed at the phenomenal growth of the Christian Church in that land which had seen so much persecution under the Japanese and under the Communists. I looked in at one church on the Sunday morning which was holding its *fifth* Sunday Morning Service and that in a church which seated 3000 people! One of the reasons, I was told, was that Christians in South Korea are trained and committed to the task of winning their fellow Koreans to Christ. So often in other lands it is left to the pastor, or the vicar or minister. 'It's his job', we say, and sit on our bottoms and do precisely nothing about others. I recall too a dream that a great preacher recounted. He imagined that he was in heaven. Gabriel, the angel, was walking with the Master who had not long returned from earth, they were talking as they walked. Gabriel was asking the Master now that the work of redemption had been completed, what plans had been made to take the message to a desperately needy world. The Master had replied, 'Well I left eleven men to whom I promised I would send the power of the Holy Spirit, and told them to be my witnesses to the uttermost parts of the earth.' 'Eleven men' exclaims Gabriel in utter amazement, 'But supposing they don't go! What other plans have you made?' To which the Master replied, 'I have had no other plans, I'm counting on them!' He has made no other plans and He is counting on you and me to do the work of winning the World to Himself. In Japan only 1% is Christian, one million out of 100 million Japanese! And yet if each of the 1,000,000 Christians took twelve months to win just one other Japanese to Christ, at the end of one year there would be two million, and if that process was repeated each year, at the end of just seven years the whole nation would be won for Christ! That is the simple strategy that God has designed, and He relies on ordinary people to carry it through. 'He has made no other plan, He is counting on us.'

Playing the second fiddle well!
'As unknown, yet well known.' 2 Cor. 6:9

I want to consider with you an aspect of spiritual experience that brings challenge and yet encouragement to many, many Christians. I want to study how again and again both in Scripture and in the story of the Church we find that there are people who while never hitting the headlines of fame, nevertheless play a strategic role, and without whose faithfulness those who do hit the headlines would never have done so!

When the time came for me to say farewell to my last congregation, that of St George's Tron in Glasgow I found myself dreading my final and farewell Sunday when for the last time I would be in the pulpit preaching to my own people. We had a very wonderful day! What made it a little easier was the fact that the 'good-byes' would not be said until the Monday evening when a farewell social gathering had been arranged to take place in the City Halls. What an unforgettable evening that proved to be! There was a wonderful crowd filling the hall and a number of speakers who said many nice things about the years of our ministry. All the four men who had served as my assistants were among them. One said something that has stuck in my mind ever since! The Rev Bill Wallace recalled how there was something that he did not find too easy to cope with during the three years that he served with me, which was that when he went visiting the members of the congregation in their homes he found that those he visited seldom spoke appreciatively about *his* sermons, but almost always about *mine*! On one occasion he called on an elderly lady. She began, 'I was watching the Minister on the telly last night. . .' He said to himself 'here we go again!' She continued . . . 'I was watching the Minister on the telly last night and I thought to myself, he's just like yersel!' Bill thought to himself 'this sounds a little more promising.' She went on, 'He's just like yerself', you've both got the same good head of hair!' That was not what he was hoping to hear! Bill then went on to add that one of the things his Father had taught him about Christian service was that one of the most important lessons to learn and to apply was that of learning to play the second fiddle well!

Think for a moment how often we come across those whose worth is seldom recognised by men, but I am sure will never be overlooked by God, and will certainly not go unrewarded. Many are prepared to recognise the prominent part played by Simon Peter among the disciples, but forget that if there had not been an Andrew who 'brought him to Jesus' there would never have been a Peter! The Church universal gives thanks to God for Paul, the greatest Christian who ever lived, but forget that if there had not been a Barnabas there might never have been a Paul! Do you recall how we read in Acts 9:26 how after his conversion, Saul, as he was then called, made his way to Jerusalem and attempted to join himself to the disciples, but we read that they were all afraid of him and believed not that he was a disciple! He found his overtures repulsed. He wasn't wanted! How easy it would have been for Saul to have turned away, to have walked out of the fellowship thinking, 'well if this is what the Christian Church is like then I don't want to have anything more to do with it.' 'But', we read, 'Barnabas took him!' Supposing there hadn't been a Barnabas, there might never have been a Paul! Take this to a still higher level, we can say reverently that before there could be a Christ on earth, there had to be a Mary! If all this is true in Scripture, then it is also true in the story of the Church all down the ages. I have had fun in my travels all over the world in asking audiences small and large if anyone present has known anything about Albert McMakin! The response has been almost inevitably been negative. But Albert was the young man who took a sixteen year old American High School boy to hear an evangelist during a mission in their home town in the States where that sixteen year old boy found Christ, and the name of that boy was Billy Graham! So before there could be a Billy there had to be an Albert!

For our study I want to look at the book of Ruth and to see how before there could be a Ruth, there had to be a Naomi, someone who played the second fiddle so well that it meant that her daughter-in-law sought and found a living faith in her mother-in-law's God!

I want to begin by noting:

How testing were the events in her life

Life was not easy for Naomi, indeed it had been the very opposite. Think of *the difficulty of her surroundings*. She had been compelled to leave Bethlehem for the land of Moab. The story is told in the opening verses in the first chapter of the book of Ruth. I cannot think that that would have made life easy for Naomi. It would have meant leaving all her friends and relatives behind and that cannot have been easy. I don't know how far the language would have been different, but the religion certainly was for we read in v15 how Orpah was described as returning to 'her gods'. The Moabites were of course traditionally hostile to the Israelites. I note the point because so often we are tempted to make the difficulty of our surroundings an excuse for lowering the standard of our Christian witness! How many Christians find themselves in situations where the going is tough and where to live a truly Christian life is far from easy! To be the only Christian teacher in the staff room. When we find ourselves in some such situation we are inclined to look enviously at others and say 'well it is all very well for him or her, but I am in a different situation altogether.' How do we know that it is all right for them! But the temptation to excuse ourselves is there!

Think too of *the intensity of her sufferings*. In addition to the hurt of leaving home and her friends came blow after blow. In v3 we are told that Naomi's husband died. The fact is recorded without comment. But what a shattering blow that must have been both financially and emotionally. Then her two sons added sorrow upon sorrow when they both married pagan wives! I have conducted hundreds of weddings and know full well that in most cases they have been times of great happiness for all concerned, but there have been times when behind the smiling faces of a bride's Father and Mother there have been broken hearts as they had felt that their daughter had been making a tragic mistake. Was that how Naomi had felt too? Then, ten years later both her sons died and Naomi was left alone! Surely that must have been the last straw. Have some of us too known what it has meant to suffer?

Whenever I think of Naomi I think of a member of my congregation at Christ Church Cockfosters. I don't suppose you would have thought of her as an outstanding person unless you had been very observant, and then you would have noticed a look of unusual serenity and peace in her face. It was some time before I learned her story. Her husband was an alcoholic, and any alcoholic turns any home into a hell. During World War Two her home in North London was hit during an air-raid one night. She lay there in the dark and dust, trapped and unable to move. Her two little girls were also trapped amid the ruins. She could not move hand or foot to help either of them and had to lie there in the dark and listen to her two girlies slowly die! She had two sons and one of them served in the Merchant Navy. One day she received a cable from Bombay, and it was to tell that there had been an accident and he was dead! I have never forgotten what she said as she ended her story. 'Mr Duncan, I had to learn that submission was not enough, there had to be acceptance.' How testing the events had been in her life, just like the events in the life of Naomi.

The second thing to note about the experience of Naomi was:

How telling was the witness to her Lord

There are two facets of this that we do well to consider, and the first is *how close was the relationship between them*, between Naomi and her two daughters-in-law. Orpah and Ruth had had ample time to watch and observe how their mother-in-law had reacted to the circumstances in her life. They had come to love her and when there was talk of parting, both of them were in tears. Ten years they had watched and that in one of the sometimes more difficult relationships in life!

The point I want to make is that the real challenge to the quality of our Christian witness will be found in the closer relationships of life. That is where the real test comes, not in the warmth of a living Christian fellowship on Sundays, but when we come down to earth with a bang in the office on the Monday, what we are in the classroom, what we are on the factory floor, in the hospital ward, in the board-room, behind the shop counter, in the home!! I remember hearing of a Christian businessman who had taken part in a religious service on Sunday night which was broadcast. One of the girls in his office had listened to her boss, she wasn't a Christian. On Monday morning when he came to his office something went wrong and he lost his temper, something he was known to do pretty often. The volcano of his wrath erupted and this girl was swamped in the flames of his anger. As she went out of the office she passed another girl coming in who wasn't a Christian either. The one going out said to the one coming in as they passed, 'That's right! On Sunday night come to Jesus. On Monday morning, go to hell!' Not much witness there! It was said of the late Fred Mitchell at the Memorial Service held in Westminster Chapel after his untimely death in the first Comet airliner crash — 'You never caught Fred Mitchell off his guard, for he never needed to be on it!' Like his Master's robe, Fred Mitchell's Christian character and testimony was woven of one piece throughout! It was true also of our blessed Lord when John wrote of Him, 'The Word was made flesh and dwelt among us, and we beheld His glory, the glory as of the only begotten Son of God, full of grace and truth.' After being as close to Jesus Christ as anyone could have been for three wonderful years, John was able to say, 'we beheld His glory!' How close was the relationship between them.

And the other thing to note is *how clear was the reality before them*. Ruth at least was convinced and her heart was won! What sweeter words have ever been spoken than those spoken by Ruth to Naomi in verses 16 and 17: 'Whither thou goest I will go and where thou lodgest I will lodge; thy people shall be my people, and thy God shall be my God.' 'Thy God shall be my God'. I find myself asking the question would anyone who knew me through and through ever want to say 'I want your God to be my God'? Would anyone who knew you through and through ever want to say the same? That is the wonder of the quality and the reality that Ruth had seen in the life of her mother-in-law!! Some years ago and when the Filey Christian Holiday Convention was held at Filey, we heard the testimony of a West German Christian, Anton Schulte. He was speaking at what was called the Late-Night Extra, the final informal gathering for the day held each evening in the Gaiety Theatre holding three thousand people. It was not his first visit to England! He had previously come to the UK as a prisoner of war during World War Two! He had spent part of his time billetted with a Christian family in Ayrshire! The quality of their lives and testimony were such that he became a Christian! One of the great evangelists in my younger days was Lionel B. Fletcher. He tells of how when he made his way to the counselling room after one of his meetings, as he entered the room he saw a lady and gentleman standing together. He made his way towards them, but when he reached them the man said, 'You don't need to tell me anything, Mr Fletcher, I've been living with it for twenty years', and he turned and smiled at his wife standing beside him!

We have been considering how testing were the events

in her life, how telling was the witness to her Lord, and finally and very wonderfully:

How thrilling was the outcome for the world

There are two aspects of this part of the story of Naomi that we have to look at for our great encouragement. We have to note *the immediage result*. Naomi's reward was rich for into the loneliness and emptiness of her heart and life came a new and believing daughter-in-law! I believe that one of the most wonderful things about being a Christian, about the life that God uses, lies in the enrichment of our lives through the other lives that God brings into our lives and blesses through the contacts we have with them. I have never forgotten how in South Africa Bishop Stephen Bradley shared with me the contents of a letter he had just received from a life-long friend of his in Australia. She was nearing the end of the road and been looking back over the years in which she had exercised a great influence on girls coming out of prison who had no-one to meet them at the prison gates and no-one to care for them! She had written to tell the Bishop that she had been doing a little bit of arithmetic. She had found that God in His mercy had blessed her quiet ministry to these girls and that there were now 1500 Christian women in full-time service in different parts of her land and others lands, whom she had first met at the prison gates! I am convinced that no-one who is living the Christian life as God meant it to be lived need ever be lonely. There will always be others that God will bring into our lives and across our paths for whom we can pray, to whom we can speak or write, for whom we can care, and show God's caring concern. We might not be much use in a pulpit, but we can use our tea-pots, our sitting-rooms! Yes the immediate result for Naomi was rewarding.

But what shall we say of *the ultimate result?* For that we have to look towards the end of the last chapter in the Book of Ruth. There we find that Naomi not only had Ruth, but when Ruth re-married, Naomi got a new son-in-law as well. But beyond that, indeed beyond

Naomi's knowledge while she lived out her days on earth was something that was to find its place in God's purpose for the whole world! The son born to Ruth and Boaz was called Obed. When he grew up and married he had a son and his name was Jesse. When Jesse grew up and married, he and his wife had among their sons a boy and and they called his name *David*! David the man after God's own heart, whose Psalms are still sung all over the world, who became the King of Israel! And all of this was the result of Naomi 'playing the second fiddle well', living such a quality of life that she won to a true faith in the Living God, her daughter-in-law Ruth. Albert McMakin never dreamt that the high-school boy for whom he prayed and whom he took to hear that evangelist was going to grow up to be the greatest evangelist the world has ever seen! The family in Ayrshire did not know that that German prisoner-of-war who found Christ through the faithfulness of their witness was going to become one of the great evangelists to the German people! But that is the way God loves to work, using ordinary people and catching them up into His great programme of reaching the whole world that He so loved and still loves, that world for which He gave His only begotten Son 'that whosoever believeth in Him should not perish but have everlasting life.' 'God', so Paul tells us, 'will have all men to be saved and come to the knowledge of the truth'. And every single Christian is meant to be caught up into that great purpose, and only eternity will reveal what God has been able to do through ordinary Christians who have learned to play the second fiddle well. Unknown, maybe on earth, but well known in heaven!

Launch out into the deep and let down your nets for a draught
Luke 5:1–11

There are some passages of the Bible that I am sure have been more meaningful than others to most of us. Whenever I think in terms of Christian service this incident recorded in Luke's Gospel leaps to my mind. I can only think that if it has been a blessing to me in my life it will be a blessing to others also. This passage always awakens two memories for me! The first is the title of a book, by a Dr Trumbull, an American. The book was titled *Taking Men Alive'*. The other memory is from a book written by another American, Dr S D Gordon. His books were all called *Quiet Talks*. They had titles like *Quiet Talks on Service*; *Quiet Talks on Power* and *Quiet Talks on Prayer*. They were called *Quiet Talks* because that was the way he spoke and preached. He never raised his voice to the best of my knowledge and I heard him speak at Keswick and also in my father's Church! If he wanted to emphasise a point he didn't raise his voice, he dropped it, almost to a whisper, saying very quietly 'Are you listening?' In one of his books, I think it must have been *Quiet Talks on Service*, he devoted a chapter to the study of this miracle of the great draught of fishes. This miracle, like all other miracles, I believe, is a parable in action. Someone once said 'all great teachers teach pictorially' and Jesus Christ was of course the greatest of all teachers and he taught pictorially! Either still pictures painted with words as parables or moving pictures in action and deeds that we call miracles. They all have at least one major lesson. So I want us to note that Christ describes the service into which he calls his disciples as 'catching men'. In Mark 1:17 He says 'Come ye after Me I will make you become fishers of men' and in verse 10 of this chapter at the end of the miracle He says to Simon Peter 'From henceforth thou shalt catch men'. Winning men to Christ, Jesus says, is like fishing! Of course there are some essential differences. Christian Service is seeking to bring men into newness of life, not to death, unless it be the death of the old life! In Christian Service we need to win the consent of those we are seeking to win. They cannot be dragged into the Kingdom, but surely brought in response to the constraint of the Holy Spirit! In ordinary fishing the bait, if fishing were by line, would deceive. In Christian Service the offering we hold forth to men is not to deceive them it is the truth! So let us look into this incident for our encouragement and our instruction.

First of all I want to note what I have called:

A request that was challenging

It was a two-fold request and it was first of all a challenge, when we think of *where they were told to go*. They were told 'Launch out *into the deep*'. I have always felt the challenge of this, and wondered quite what it meant. Did the 'deep' mean the unexpected, the unlikely place? Some fishermen would say that you don't catch fish in the deeper waters, but in the shallower waters; so this was a challenge to go out to the unlikely, the unexpected place. That line of thought is suggestive is it not and sometimes God calls us to serve and seek amongst unexpected people, unlikely places. Recently I heard on the radio of a vicar who concentrated his efforts to win a man to faith in Christ who was a manager of a 'sex shop'! It took a long time but in the end the man was won.

Maybe it is not so much the unexpected and unlikely as the unexplored. Tell me is it not true, that too often there is so little depth in so much of our Christian life and service. Are there not depths of Christian knowledge and the Word of God we need to explore? This would mean we would be able to speak much more readily and much more confidently about our faith than maybe we are as yet.

Tell me, are there not depths of prayer that we need to explore. So much of what we call prayer can scarcely be called praying. So many of us have not really got much further than the kind of prayers we prayed when we were little children. A short, brief prayer — 'God bless Mummy and Daddy' and then the names of our brothers and sisters and ending with 'make me a good boy' or 'a good girl'. There is surely more to prayer than that, although the simplicity of the children's prayer *is* prayer. But when Paul prayed he likened it to travail. When Christ prayed there were times when He knew what it was to be in an agony. When Jesus was teaching His disciples about prayer He likened it to hammering on a door at midnight. Are there, then, depths of prayer we need to explore?

What about depths of giving? Is there a shallow superficiality here? So often we give to God what we would not give as a tip to someone who has rendered us a service. So often we are prepared to spend on a meal far, far more than we would ever dream of putting into the collection on Sunday. So much Christian work in so many areas of the world is crippled for lack of money. Someone once said God has asked for a seventh of our time, and a tenth of our money! I wonder how many Christians reach that kind of standard of stewardship?

Tell me are there not depths of obedience? Obedience which will lead us to share our faith with someone whom we know. Maybe obedience which will mean we will give more of our time, showing God's concern for people we do not know. An obedience which will open our lips, call for sacrifice and inconvenience in our pattern of living. There was a challenge then in where they were told to go.

There was also *a challenge in what they were told to use*. The equipment that was to be used was theirs. 'Let down *your* nets'. How many Christians wait for the vicar or pastor to let down *his* net? Or they wait for the coming of a great evangelist like Dr Billy Graham and expect him to let down *his* net. Now of course vicars and pastors are involved and I myself am 100% for evangelism along the pattern followed by Dr Billy Graham. Given the right man and the right time God unquestionably sets His seal upon it and I have never been able to understand those who hold back. But the real way of winning men comes when we *all* let down *our* nets.

I am never tired of quoting Dr Paul Rees, who said once, 'Every Christian lives at the centre of expanding circles of contact'. What about your home and mine? Haven't we ever dreamed of using our homes in the service of God, inviting not just our congenial friends to come but to invite others, neighbours, people we do not know so well? What about your job? The contacts we have where we work, people we get to know and above all who get to know us. What about your personality.

God made you to be you. You may be rather shy and don't find it too easy to speak. Well, maybe you're a good listener, and the world needs listeners desperately. Everyone of us has a different personality, different natural gifts, different spiritual gifts, what about these? I believe God's challenge to the Christian Church today is to every Christian '*Let down your nets*'. The challenge in the request that was made. The challenge lay in where they were told to go and in what they were told to use!

Secondly I think it is worth noting what I have called:

The response that was faltering

We read in verse 5 that Simon Peter answering said unto Him 'Master we have toiled all the night and taken nothing. Nevertheless at Thy word I will let down the net'. Note *the reluctance that Peter showed*. Peter was just not in the mood to do the will of his Lord, and so he raises objections. I wonder whether he thought he knew more about fishing than his Master? Or just that they had indeed toiled all night and had taken nothing and were tired and did not want to make any more effort, so he makes excuses. Just like we do when we face the challenge of our spiritual responsibility to others. But what I find encouraging in my Bible is that so often it is the people that do object, who do try to get out of it, who do make excuses that are the very people God does use. God never uses those who are cock-sure and confident.

You remember what happened when God called Moses. Moses was a man who had settled down to a quiet life looking after sheep and God wanted him to deliver a nation! In Exodus chapters 3 and 4 we read of that encounter he had with the living God. Moses was full of excuses. In Exodus 3:11 we read 'Who am I that I should go?' In verse 13 of the same chapter he says 'What shall I say?' In chapter 4, verse 1 he objects 'They will not believe me'. In verse 10 of that chapter he objects again 'I am not eloquent, I cannot speak' and in verse 1 of that chapter he tries the final way of escape 'Send, I pray thee, someone else'. Full of excuses and yet that was the very man that God was going to use.

It was the same when God called Gideon to deliver his nation, in his time. Do you remember what Gideon said 'Wherewithal shall I save Israel? My family is poor, I am the youngest in the family'? When God called Jeremiah it was just the same. In Jeremiah Ch. 1 verse 6 we read 'Then said I, Oh Lord God behold I cannot speak, for I am a child', and so with Peter it was just the same, a reluctant and hesitant obedience! I am not really concerned about the reason for that reluctance but what I am concerned about is that you and I should take note of the fact that sometimes we do raise objections, we do make excuses to opt out of our responsibility. Maybe your protest is like Peter's, you are saying 'Well, I've tried before and nothing happened'. The reluctance he showed!

But fortunately the story did not end there, and we go on to note *the obedience that Peter gave*. What wonderful words these are 'Nevertheless, *at Thy Word I will* let down the nets'. 'At Thy word I will', I believe these five words if they were taken up by every single believing Christian could bring revival to the Church almost overnight. It was the great Charles Finney who once said 'Revival consists in a new obedience'. Sometimes in my world travels and my nationwide ministry I feel as I face a congregation of Christian believers that the great need is not that they should learn anything new but rather that they should become obedient to the truth they already understand. The importance of obedience was underscored in my own life on the occasion of my first visit to the great Keswick convention. I was not a speaker, I was an assistant Scout master and we were camping on a hill called Windy Brow, on the side of a hill called Latrigg. We understood why it was called Windy Brow as we were nearly blown off the site!

In those days, prior to World War Two, the convention went on for two weekends and on the Sunday afternoon of the second weekend there was a testimony meeting and people were asked to bear testimony to what God had taught them during the convention. On the

Saturday I was cornered by Mr J M Waite, the then secretary of the convention and he asked me to speak at that testimony meeting. My problem was that I had nothing specific to say! However, on that last Sunday morning I worshipped in the Methodist Church in Southey Street. The preacher was Canon St John Thorpe. He spoke on 'Five Whatsoevers of the Christian Life,' and the first was 'The Whatsoever of Christian obedience'. He spoke of the words of Mary to the servants at the wedding at Cana of Galilee. Do you remember what she said to them, referring them to Jesus Christ, 'Whatsoever He sayeth to you, do it.' 'The What-soever of Christian obedience!' I wonder whether this is the great problem really in the Christian Church today. It must of course be 'At Thy word'. Then we follow with the 'I will', 'I will pray', 'I will give', 'I will study', 'I will go', 'I will speak', 'I will write', 'I will stop', 'At Thy word I will'. Two little phrases about obedience come to mind. The first is obedience means at once! The second is delayed obedience is disobedience!

We have considered the request that was challenging, the response that was faltering and finally let us note:

The result that was staggering

There were two comments to make here. First of all to look at the *extent of the success*. Peter had never seen anything like it before. Their nets were breaking, their boats were sinking. Partners had to be called to help. It was a story of bulging nets and sinking ships! This speaks to me of something that most of us have never seen, real revival and effective Christian service. How wonderful it must be when we see God working in this kind of way.

This is what lies behind the cry of Isaiah the prophet. 'Oh that thou wouldst render the heavens that thou wouldst come down, that the mountains would flow down at thy presence', Isaiah 64:1. And what of the cry of the psalmist, 'Wilt thou not revive us again, that thy people may rejoice in thee?' Here we have the prayer to God that seeks revival, we have the power of God that marks revival, we have the praise to God that crowns revival and above all the presence of God that is revival! When revival came to the Church of Murray McCheyne in Dundee we are told that 'evening classes in the school room were changed into densely crowded congregations in the Church and for nearly four months it was found desirable to have public worship every night.' When revival came to Wales at the beginning of this century we are told 'the prayer meetings are so crowded that the places of worship are inadequate to contain them. Some last hours with no cessation in prayer or singing'. I wonder if God is waiting for us to be more obedient so that He may be able to show us what He can do through an obedient Church.

We have noticed the extent of the success and we end by noticing the *effect of the success*, and that was not that Simon Peter went about bragging about his catch or about the wonderful fisherman he was. Instead we find the man who a few moments before had been on his feet arguing with Jesus is broken now and is on his knees at the feet of Jesus saying 'Depart from me for I am a sinful man O Lord'. Let us be under no illusion. If God is going to use us as I pray He will, that will not result in our thinking what wonderful Christians we are, but rather we shall find ourselves utterly amazed that such unworthy Christians, such sinful Christians as we are, could have any part at all in the work of God. If you read the lives of the great saints you will find this to be true. They are men and women who knew what it was constantly to be not so much on their feet praising God as on their knees worshipping Him. Remember what happened when Joshua found himself confronted by the Divine Captain before Jericho! We are told that he fell on his face! When Isaiah saw his Lord and God high and lifted up we read that he said 'Woe is me, I am undone, I am a sinful man'! When John in Revelation chapter 1 saw the risen and ascended Lord in His glory we read that he said 'When I saw Him I fell at His feet as one dead'!

I remember very vividly on one occasion being told by one of the senior speakers at Keswick, when I myself